SCOTNOTES
Number 12

The Poetry of
William Dunbar

by

Ronald D.S. Jack

Professor of Scottish & Medieval Literature
University of Edinburgh

Association for Scottish Literary Studies 1997

Published by
Association for Scottish Literary Studies
9 University Gardens
University of Glasgow
Glasgow G12 8QH

First published 1997

© Ronald D.S. Jack 1997

A CIP catalogue for this title is available from the British Library

ISBN 0 948877 32 4

Subsidised by

THE SCOTTISH ARTS COUNCIL

Typeset by Roger Booth Associates, Hassocks, West Sussex
Printed by BPC AUP Aberdeen Ltd

CONTENTS

Editors' Foreword   iv
Note on References   v

Introduction: Approaching Dunbar   1

Chapter One: At the Court of James IV   3
'On His Heid-ake', 'Complaint to the King aganis Mure', 'Of the Warldis Instabilitie', 'To Aberdein', 'Of a Dance in the Quenis Chalmer', *'The Thrissil and the Rois'*, *'The Wowing of the King quhen he wes in Dunfermline'*, *'Of the Warldis Vanitie'*.

    Further Study   10

Chapter Two: Message and Medium: 'To the Merchantis of Edinburgh'   12
'To the Merchantis of Edinburgh'.

Chapter Three: The Ladder of Style: Devilishness, Death and Damian   22
'Ane Remonstrance to the King', *'The Fenyeit Freir of Tungland'*, *'The Lament for the Makaris'*, *'Ane Ballat of Our Lady'*.

    Further Study   36

Chapter Four: Form and Meaning: Of 'Targe' and 'Tretis' [51–85]   38
'The Goldyn Targe', *'The Tretis of the Twa Mariit Wemen and the Wedo'*.

    Further Study   60

Poems indicated in italics are treated at length.
Non-italicised poems are only referred to.

EDITORS' FOREWORD

The *Scotnotes* booklets are a series of study guides to major Scottish writers and literary texts that are likely to be elements within literature courses. They are aimed at senior pupils in secondary schools and students in further education colleges and colleges of education. Consequently it is intended that, wherever possible, each booklet in the series will be written by a person who is not only an authority on the particular writer or text but also experienced in teaching at the relevant levels in schools or colleges. Furthermore, the editorial board, composed of members of the Schools and Further Education Committee of the Association for Scottish Literary Studies, considers the suitability of each booklet for the students in question. In preparing the series, the editors are conscious of the fact that for many years there has been a shortage of readily accessible critical notes for the general student of Scottish literature; and they intend that *Scotnotes* will grow as a series at the rate of about two booklets a year to meet this need and provide students with valuable aids to the understanding and appreciation of the key writers and major texts within the Scottish literary tradition.

Lorna Borrowman Smith
Elaine Petrie

NOTE ON REFERENCES

All page references within parentheses in this study guide are to *The Poems of William Dunbar*, edited by W. MacKay MacKenzie (reprinted Edinburgh, 1990).

INTRODUCTION

Approaching Dunbar

To introduce a late-medieval poet who prides himself on the skilfulness of his verse provides writer and reader with a triple challenge. Some attempt to recreate the poet's world – in this case the court of James IV and Margaret Tudor – is necessary. Dunbar's use of Middle Scots has to be discussed. Finally, the rules and conventions governing his art need to be understood.

I have organised the discussion around these issues. Inevitably, historical, linguistic and literary questions will overlap. Chapter One, however, focuses primarily on the Scotland of the late fifteenth century; Chapter Two emphasises language; Chapter Three covers the full stylistic range of Dunbar's poetry; while Chapter Four looks at the different forms he employs in approaching the theme of love. Throughout, representative poems have been chosen to explain the topic under consideration, allowing in-depth analysis. Guidance to other works in the same mode is provided at the end of the relevant chapter.

The primary aim is to allow readers to enjoy Dunbar. There is no need to justify him qualitatively. With Robert Burns and Hugh MacDiarmid, he is one of the three finest lyric poets Scotland has produced. Indeed, MacDiarmid advised versifiers of the future to imitate this fifteenth-century courtier rather than Burns.

Essentially, all that is needed to begin your own sampling is this booklet plus access to a copy of Dunbar. The best, but very expensive, edition is *The Poems of William Dunbar*, edited by James Kinsley (Oxford, 1979). My textual references, therefore, relate to and my quotations are based upon the 1990, Mercat Press reprint of *The Poems of William Dunbar*, edited by W. MacKay MacKenzie (London, 1932).

If, as I earnestly hope, you come to share my own love of and admiration for this 'poet's poet', Kinsley's text and notes should be your next port of call. An initial step in further critical reading is *A History of Scottish Literature*, edited by Cairns Craig, 4 vols. (Aberdeen, 1987; 1989). The first volume, *Medieval and Renaissance Literature*, edited by R.D.S. Jack, provides a wider literary context as well as essays on language and on Dunbar himself. The latest and most thorough critical biography is Priscilla Bawcutt's *William Dunbar* (Oxford, 1994). A short but good introduction to the Scots language is *Why Scots Matters* by J. Derrick McClure

(Edinburgh: Saltire Society, 1988). Historically, Gordon Donaldson's *Scottish Kings* (London, 1967) will introduce you to James IV economically and well. Those who wish to read about the reign in more detail should consult N.A.T. Macdougall's *James IV* (Edinburgh, 1989).

R.D.S.J.

CHAPTER ONE

At the Court of James IV

Dunbar was born in the early 1460s; he died in 1520 or shortly afterwards. His most recent biographers believe that he attended the University of St Andrews and was initially bound for the priesthood. But he provides a fair amount of autobiographical comment in his own writing. For a modern author to refer to himself in his or her fiction would not be unusual but medieval artists believed that God was the originator of all. They credited divinity with their skills, remaining modestly silent about any part they might have played in the creative procedure themselves.

Not so Dunbar. Centred at the court of James IV, he lets everyone know when he does not feel fit for work. 'On His Heid-ake'[1] begins like a modern sick-note:

> My heid did yak yester nicht,
> This day *to mak* that I na micht,
>   So sair the magryme dois me menyie,
>   Perseing my brow as ony ganyie,
> That scant I luik may on the licht.
>
> (p. 3, lines 1–5)
>
> [My head ached so much last night that I could not *compose* to-day. So sorely does headache grip me, piercing through my forehead like an arrow, that I can scarcely bear to look out on the daylight.][2]

When other poets interfere with his work, he does not see the outrage as committed against God but against William Dunbar. In 'Complaint to the King Aganis Mure', a well-known Edinburgh beggar and vagabond of the time, he voices his personal fury directly:

> Schir, I complane off injuris:
> A refing sonne off rakyng MURIS
> Hes magellit *my making* throw his malis.
>
> (p. 5, lines 1–3)
>
> [Sir, I complain that I've been injured; a thieving son of the beggar Mure's family has maliciously mangled my *work*.]

What do these pained exclamations tell us?

As my italicising highlights, Dunbar views himself first and foremost as a poet or 'maker'. Early Scots writers all described themselves as 'Makars'. This reveals a down-to-earth view of art. The poet 'makes' word structures as a builder builds with bricks. Hard labouring is involved. The poet must also have the knowledge of the architect. Like the latter, he has to consider how the various pieces and pressures of his verbal house or cathedral will come together.

Dunbar also reveals that he works under patronage. 'Schir' betrays the lot of the commissioned poet. He is vulnerable because others determine his pay. The most frequent topic of his many poetic lamentations reflects this insecurity. With his priestly background, he thinks he warrants a regular salary in the form of an ecclesiastical living or 'benefice'. A poem which begins 'This waverand warldis wretchidnes' ('The wretchedness of this everchanging world')[3] identifies the major symptom of that world's misery eleven stanzas later:

> I knaw nocht how the kirk is gydit,
> Bot beneficis ar nocht leill devydit;
> Sum men hes sevin, and I nocht ane;
>   Quhilk to considder is ane pane.
>
> (p. 30, lines 45–8)
>
> [I don't know how the Kirk is organised, but benefices are not shared out fairly; some men have seven and I not one; it's a pain to think about that.]

Metaphysical mayhem exists because one Scottish poet is being unfairly treated.

A second implication of patronage is the commissioning of verse. As Dunbar's principal patrons were King James IV and Queen Margaret, he often had to assume a politically correct voice. When, in 'To Aberdein', he apostrophises that city as the 'beryl above all other towns' ('thow beriall of all tounis', p. 137) he may be using the jewel image because he really believes it to be the brightest or purest of Scottish towns. Quite certainly, he has been ordered to write verses for Queen Margaret's visit to Aberdeen in May 1511 and wants to fill a purse whose empty state, he elsewhere admits, pricks at him like a hedgehog's spines.[4]

The personal bias may also be explained chronologically. The need to be humble before God, the first 'Makar' (Creator/Artist), had been accepted without question by most poets in medieval Scotland. Dunbar belongs to the late Middle Ages and early Renaissance, when more attention is being paid to the individual.

This is, in the words of Dunbar's older contemporary Robert Henryson, to 'excuse als far furth as I may', but the impression remains that Dunbar called pitying attention to himself so often because he was a moaner by nature. He was not of noble birth. Physically, he was small – a rival poet calls him a 'dearch' (dwarf). Such disadvantages would not help him in imposing his own high opinion of himself on others. Nor, as he admits, did it make him a success with women. In 'Of a Dance in the Quenis Chalmer', he visualises himself capering clumsily at a party held in the Queen's apartments:

> Than cam in Dunbar the Mackar;
> On all the flure thair was nane frackar,
> And thair he dancet the dirrye dantoun;
> He hoppet lyk a pillie wanton,
>   For luff of Musgraeffe, men tellis me;
> He trippet, quhill he tint his panton:
>   A mirrear dance mycht na man se.
>
>   (p. 61, lines 22–8)

[Then Dunbar the poet came in; there was none more smartly got up on the entire floor, and there he danced the Dirrye Dantoun (one of the more energetic dances of the day) hopping about like a wanton colt – out of love for Lady Musgrave, I'm told. He tripped about until he lost his dancing slipper: a merrier dance was never witnessed.]

'Of a Dance' consists of a series of exaggerated portraits. The senior poet presents six courtiers and the queen's dog with a verbal cartoon of themselves in action. While these verbal 'stills' are all intended to amuse, his vision of himself as unsuccessful suitor and tiny, over-enthusiastic dancer reminds us that the tones of self-pity and paranoia are never far distant from Dunbar's verse.

One has to be careful when using such a mind to mirror James IV's court. Those elements within it, which most affected the lot of the makar, will loom disproportionately high. Historians may welcome the king's desire to make the courts at Edinburgh and Stirling centres of European culture; Dunbar will remain aggrieved because the policy introduces foreign competition. Historians may approve James's involvement in the new sciences; Dunbar thought this a waste of public money. The public purse should pour its 'silver sorrow' ('To the King', p. 1) over the servants of culture and William Dunbar in particular rather than chemists, physicists or doctors.

By definition, Dunbar's perspective will also tend to be conservative. Someone paid by the Stewart royal family could not afford to be too radical in his thinking. On the other hand, senior professional poets in Scotland had bardic licence. In part court jesters, they could also authoritatively voice those warnings necessary for the survival of the tribe. This is why Dunbar's public poem celebrating the marriage of James to Margaret Tudor – 'The Thrissil and the Rois' – can include criticism of the king's lustfulness. As bard and father figure he has the licence to voice unpopular truths, even if he veils them in flower symbolism. The Thistle-King of Scotland must

> Not hald non udir flour in sic denty
> As the fresche Ros of cullour reid and quhyt;
> For gife thow dois, hurt is thyne honesty.
>
> (p. 111, lines 141–3)
>
> [Do not hold any other flower in the same esteem as the fresh Rose (= Queen Margaret) of colours red and white (the English Tudor roses of Lancaster and York); because – if you do that – you hurt your own (reputation for) honesty.]

Before the invention of the printing press, most verse was written to be read or sung aloud. Much of it was performed. When, in 'Meditation in Wyntir', Dunbar adds Winter's dark nights and bad weather to migraine ('the magryme') as an excuse for not meeting deadlines, he describes his non-existent work as songs, ballads and plays ('sangis, ballattis and... playis', p. 26, line 5). Dunbar's poem for the royal wedding, 'The Thrissil and the Rois', was probably all three in one. That poem may conveniently introduce us to the coterie within which he worked.

The title links the heraldic symbols of Scotland (thistle) and England (rose) but the political union, so idyllically celebrated, was actually a product of plot and counter-plot. James had earlier offered himself and his crown in marriage union to Spain. He still maintained the Auld Alliance with France. In marrying the daughter of Henry VII of England, he was dramatically changing foreign policy by turning his most inveterate enemy into his father-in-law.

Dunbar uses the imagery of heraldry to de-personalise the issue. The red-haired James becomes, in the poet's dream vision, not only the thistle but also the red lion rampant set on a field of gold, the Royal Arms of the Scottish Crown ('Reid of his cullour, as is the ruby glance; On feild of gold he stude full mychtely,' p. 110, lines 96–97). Foreign policy is translated into a world of plants and heraldry. The lion image reminds Dunbar's audience that James rules – like the king of beasts – in a hierarchical society, working down from God through king to nobles and then ordinary people. The Court may be a small group but it controls the country's fate.

This places a weighty responsibility on the shoulders of a poet, who welcomes such an event on behalf of his fellow countrymen. Dunbar knew James IV's strengths. He was one of the most learned Scottish monarchs. Pedro da Ayala, the Spanish ambassador, noted admiringly that he spoke Latin, French, Flemish, German, Spanish and Gaelic. He had also mastered Danish. He was courageous, far-sighted and worked hard at the job of kingship.

Yet he was also a man of extremes, and the promiscuity, which Dunbar criticises in his poem, has a firm base in fact. Margaret Tudor was fragile, as the rose imagery suggests, because she had barely reached her teens when she became the bride of a king in his mid-twenties with a reputation as a womaniser. The names of Marion Boyd, Margaret Drummond and Janet Kennedy form the list of known royal mistresses between 1495 and 1498. James IV was still paying for the support of his daughter by Margaret Drummond when he married. He maintained mother and daughter in apartments in Stirling until 1508 at least.

Margaret Tudor would not remain vulnerable for long! A strong, wilful personality, she played her own part in turning the imagined heaven of the marriage into an actual hell. From her Stirling court, she sought to vie with James in dalliance. The dance in her chambers, described earlier, confirms her worldliness. But she was also of royal blood and had inherited an imperial cast of mind, as Dunbar reminds us in 'To the Princess Margaret':

> Younge tender plant of pulcritud,
> Descendyd of Imperyalle blude.
> (p. 178, lines 5–6)
>
> [Young, tender, beauteous plant, descended from the blood of rulers.]

This conflict of wills between Stewart and Tudor ushered in a sixteenth century which would witness the even more bitter battle between Mary, Queen of Scots and Elizabeth I.

Noble women were not the only ones to attract the king. In 'The Wowing (wooing) of the King quhen he was in Dunfermline', Dunbar depicts his monarch-patron roughly seducing a peasant girl. It is impossible to assess how James would have reacted to a poem which shows him using his power to terrorise and, eventually, rape the girl. To a twentieth-century audience, the monarch's behaviour is criminal and the poet's outrage seems clear. In the fifteenth century, the social order favoured masculinity and authority, while the king's privileged position might have blinded him to the darker implications of this beast-fable.

In 'The Wowyng', the red-haired king is transformed into a red fox and the girl into a lamb. As the fox was, in fable and bestiary, a type of the devil and the lamb stood for innocence, the choice of animals, in itself, implies disapproval of the king's behaviour. As a member of the under-privileged classes, raised to the courtly level by his power over words, Dunbar must have understood the girl's position. As king's poet, he was certainly not paid to insult his patron. These personal tensions carry through into the lyric. On one level, it may be taken as a piece of upper class male bawdry, on another (and more powerfully) it depicts a country where strength may overrule morality:

> He grippit hir abowt the west,
> And handlit hir as he had hest;
> This innocent, that nevir trespast.
>
> (p. 52, lines 29–31)
>
> [He (wolf/James) seized her (lamb/girl) round the waist and handled her roughly as he was in a hurry; this innocent, who had never sinned.][5]

James IV's extreme character balanced this lustiness with a sombre form of religious seriousness. Drawn into the rebellion which resulted in the death of his father James III, he retained a sense of guilt for that involvement. He is reported to have worn an iron belt next to his skin to mortify the flesh. Regularly, he went on penitential retreats and pilgrimages.

Dunbar sums up the reasons for such behaviour concisely in 'Of the Warldis Vanitie'. The second stanza reads:

> Walk furth, pilgrame, quhill thow hes dayis lycht,
>   Dres fra desert, draw to thy duelling place;
> Speid home, for quhy anone cummis the nicht,
>   Quhilk dois the follow with ane ythand chaise;
> 5 Bend up thy saill and win thy port of grace;
> For, and the deith ourtak the in trespas,
>   Than may thow say thir wourdis with 'allace!'
> *Vanitas Vanitatum, et omnia Vanitas.*
>
> (p. 151, lines 9–16)

> [Forward, pilgrim, while you still possess the day's light; leave the desert, approach your dwelling place; hurry home because night soon comes, chasing you relentlessly; tighten your sails and gain your harbour of grace for, if death overtake you while in a state of sin, then you may well lament aloud in these words: *Vanity, vanity, all is vanity*.]

This stanza not only provides an important spiritual counterbalance to James IV's enthusiasm for worldly pleasures, it turns temporal power into a day's rule under God (1–4). The Latin refrain (8) reminds the listener that the joys of an earthly king's domain are only vanities.

The idea of the spiritual journey or pilgrimage differs from the normal geographical idea of a journey as physical movement from point 'a' to point 'b' in at least three ways. All of them are depicted in the stanza cited.

(1) The journey of the pilgrim is into a strange land from which he returns to his true home. Similarly, our stay on earth is in a foreign land or an inn. Our true home is in heaven. In imagining the pilgrim rushing back home across the desert to his true dwelling place, Dunbar enacts the joyous truth that Death can only end our exile and release us into heaven (1–2).

(2) As the chase ends in the 'port of grace' (heaven), so the spiritual journey transcends all our frantic movements in this world. Our end is, willingly, to cease willing and chasing. It is night which chases the ship of life; the frantic tightening of the sail does not prevent Death overtaking. But it does so not in a literal but a divine harbour of grace, where the pilgrim safely rests. He has, as it were, handed his baton to God, who will reward him on a different plane (3–4).

(3) The pilgrim may do this because the journey from birth to death provides time to prepare oneself morally and spiritually for the afterlife. The true action is internal, the true test concerns the soul. Dunbar's pilgrim is only truly defeated by Death if his soul is in a sinful state ('in trespas') (6–7).

The penitential belt, the spiritual journeys and religious retreats undergone by James IV bear witness to his acceptance of these theological and ethical re-definitions of life's journey. The Latin refrain, lamenting the vanity of worldly possessions (8), was often chanted in church services. For James, it would at once remind him of his humble rôle as God's caretaker within the realm of vanities and provide reassurance that proper penance would erase the guilt he felt over his father's death.

For us, it serves as a reminder that Dunbar, for all his concern with money and fame, is also a devoutly Christian poet. In Chapters 3 and 4, his full poetic range from intricate hymns to worldly satire will be traced but the middle ground must detain us first. In Chapter Two, our own journey moves geographically beyond the court, sociologically into the middle classes and linguistically into a detailed study of Middle Scots as represented by the middle style.[6]

Suggestions for Further Readings and Study:

(1) Dunbar on Dunbar
Dunbar's personal insecurity is reflected in a large number of lyrics concerned with the opinions of others. All of these focus criticism through a refrain, repeated with or without minor variation, at the end of each stanza. 'Of the Warldis Instabilitie' with its anti-climatic refrain 'Quhilk to consider is ane pane' was discussed in Chapter One. It stands at the centre of this group, which also contains 'How Sall I Governe Me' (p. 24). The refrain of this lyric, 'How sould I governe me?', is a cry of despair emerging from the poet's discovery that any form of behaviour he adopts – happy or sad, ostentatious or understated – is maliciously interpreted. 'Of Deming' (p. 23), 'Of Discretioun in Asking' (p. 31) and 'The Petition of the Gray Horse, Auld Dunbar' (p. 46) share the same broad theme and the device of the witty refrain. How does Dunbar produce interesting variations on a theme rather than tedious repetition of the same modes and satirical methods?

(2) The Poet: Facts, Ideas and Fictions
The definition of poetry in the Middle Ages began with a distinction between the 'makar' and the historian. The poet could represent facts like the historian but he was not tied to them. His freedom lay in two directions – he could use his verse to imagine what *might be* rather than what was and he could use specific cases to teach general ideas. In Chapter One, 'To the King', 'The Thrissil and the Rois' and 'The Wowyng of the King quhen he wes in Dunfermline' are all based on historical facts but move into the realms of teaching and imagining. MacKay MacKenzie places the poem, 'How Dunbar wes Desyrd to be Ane Freir' (p. 3) in 'Personal Poems', although it also provides a satirical commentary on the state of the Church. Its dream form, imagined argument and devilish conclusion show, in an extreme way, how facts (personal and

historical) may at once be stated, revised and transformed. It could be used as a means of exploring how Dunbar can straddle the worlds of 'is', 'might be' and 'ought to be'.

Some of his many appeals for a 'benefice' or ecclesiastical living could then be used to test any provisional conclusions drawn from that study. 'Quhone Mony Benefices Vakit' (p. 27), 'To the King' (p. 41), 'Welcome to the Lord Treasurer' (p. 49) and 'The Birth of Antichrist' (p. 70), for example, dramatise, briefly and lyrically, the different fancies and ideas which emerge from Dunbar's actual longing for this form of financial reward.

Notes
1. MacKay MacKenzie gives titles even when there is no editorial authority for so doing. This convenient teaching practice has been followed.
2. The translations aim to combine accuracy with the degree of freedom necessary to make them immediately understandable to a twentieth-century reader. Occasionally, as here, I use italicisation to emphasise a point in the critical discussion.
3. MacKay MacKenzie, 'Of The Warldis Instabilitie', p. 28.
4. The refrain of 'To the King' (p. 1) – 'My panefull purs so priclis me' – uses this image.
5. MacKay MacKenzie's gloss of 'hest' as 'wish' is misleading. 'Trespast' has the same sense as in one version of the Lord's Prayer.
6. The high, middle and low styles will be fully defined and discussed in Chapter Two.

CHAPTER TWO

Message and Medium: 'To the Merchantis of Edinburgh'

To carry the background study beyond the court while offering guidance on Middle Scots is to set two different goals. Both may, however, be attained by studying one poem. 'To the Merchantis of Edinburgh' is printed in full below. In view of the linguistic purpose it is serving, the editorial principles of normalisation and modernisation followed elsewhere have not been employed. The text is Middle Scots with its difficulties undisguised. It has been re-edited and therefore will, at points, differ from MacKay MacKenzie's edition.

The translation is designed accurately to convey the general sense. The stricter, literal meaning of particular words and phrases is discussed, where relevant, in the analyses which follow.

TEXT:

'To the Merchantis of Edinburgh'

1. Quhy will ȝe[1] merchantis of renoun
Lat Edinburgh, ȝour nobill toun,
For laik of reformatioun
The commone proffeit tyine and fame?
   Think ȝe not schame,
That onie uther regioun
Sall with dishonour hurt ȝour name?

   [Why will you honourable merchants let your noble town of Edinburgh betray the common good and its own honourable reputation through lack of reforms? Are you not ashamed that any other region may hurtfully dishonour your good name because of this?]

2. May nane pas throw ȝour principall gaittis
For stink of haddockis and of scaittis,
For cryis of carlingis and debaittis,
For fensum flyttingis of defame;
   Think ȝe not schame,
Befoir strangeris of all estaittis
That sic dishonour hurt ȝour name?

   [Nobody can pass down your main streets because of the stench of haddocks and skates, not to mention the shouts and arguments of old hags and their offensive, defamatory name-calling; are you not ashamed that, in front of visitors from all ranks, your good name may be hurtfully dishonoured in this way?]

3. ȝour stinkand styll that standis dirk
    Haldis the lycht fra ȝour parroche kirk;
    ȝour foirstair makis ȝour housis mirk
    Lyk na cuntray bot heir at hame;
      Think ȝe not schame,
    Sa litill polesie to wirk
    In hurt and sklander of ȝour name?

    [Your stinking alley (leading into the luckenbooths) is dark, depriving your parish church of light; your outside stairs, known in no country but this one, keep your houses in shadow; are you not ashamed at having made so few improvements that your good name is hurtfully slandered?]

4. At ȝour hie croce, quhar gold and silk
    Sould be, thair is bot crudis and milk;
    And at ȝour trone bot cokill and wilk,
    Pansches, pudingis of Jok and James;
      Think ȝe not schame,
    Sen as the world sayis that ilk
    In hurt and sclander of ȝour name?

    [At your high cross, where gold and silk should be, only curds and milk are to be seen and, at your weighing beam, cockles and whelks, tripe and offal puddings sold by Tom, Dick and Harry; are you not ashamed, since the whole world is telling that same story, to the hurtful slandering of your good name?]

5. ȝour commone menstrallis hes no tone
    Bot 'Now the day dawis' and 'Into Joun';
    Cunningar men may serve Sanct Cloun
    And nevir to uther craftis clame;
      Think ȝe not schame,
    To hald sic mowaris on the moyne
    In hurt and sclander of ȝour name?

    [Your public minstrels know no tunes other than 'Now the day dawns' and 'We're in June now'; more knowledgeable people serve St Clown and never lay claim to other skills; are you not ashamed to maintain such criers-to-the-moon to the hurt and slander of your good name?]

6.   Tailȝouris, soutteris and craftis vyll
        The fairest of ȝour streittis dois fyll,
        And merchandis at the stinkand styll
        Ar hamperit in ane hony came;
            Think ȝe not schame,
        That ȝe have nether witt nor wyll
        To win ȝourselff ane bettir name?

[Tailors, cobblers and other base crafts defile the most attractive of your streets and merchants in that stinking alley are cramped as if in a honeycomb; are you not ashamed that you have neither the knowledge nor the will to gain a better name for yourselves?]

7.   ȝour burgh of beggeris is ane nest;
        To schout, thai swentȝouris will not rest;
        All honest folk they do molest,
        Sa piteuslie thai cry and rame;
            Think ȝe not schame,
        That for the poore hes nothing drest,
        In hurt and sclander of ȝour name?

[Your town is a nest of beggars; these rogues never cease shouting; they trouble all honest folk, so piteously do they cry and scream; are you not ashamed that you have devised nothing on behalf of the poor to the hurt and slander of your good name?]

8.   ȝour proffeit daylie dois incres,
        ȝour godlie workis les and les;
        Through streittis nane may mak progres
        For cry of cruikit, blind and lame;
            Think ȝe not schame,
        That ȝe sic substance dois posses
        And will nocht win ane bettir name?

[Your own monetary profit increases daily, your acts of charity become fewer and fewer; nobody may advance through the streets because of the cries of the deformed, the blind and the lame; are you not ashamed that you possess such wealth yet do not wish to win a better name?]

9.   Sen for the Court and the Sessioun,
        The great repair of this regioun
        Is in ȝour burgh, thairfoir be boun
        To mend all faultis that ar to blame;
            And eschew schame;
        Gif thai pas to ane uther toun
        ȝe will decay, and ȝour great name.

[As the siting of the law courts has made your burgh the main focal point of the region, you are duty bound to remedy all faults where blame can be proved and avoid shame; if the law courts pass to another town, your great name and you along with it will decay.]

10. Thairfoir strangeris and leigis treit,
    Tak not ouer mekill for thair meit,
    And gar ʒour merchandis be discreit;
    That na extortiounes be, proclame
        All fraud and schame;
    Keip ordour and poore nighbouris beit,
    That ʒe may gett ane bettir name.

[Therefore, deal honestly with strangers and loyal subjects alike; do not take more than is fitting and do your bargaining discreetly; openly outlaw all extortions, all fraudulent and shameful activity, keep order and assist poor neighbours, so that you may gain a better name.]

11. Singular proffeit so dois ʒow blind,
    The common proffeit gois behind;
    I pray that Lord remeid to fynd,
    That deit into Jerusalem,
        And gar ʒow schame;
    That sum tyme ressoun may ʒow bind
    For to retane for ʒow guid name.

[Personal profit so blinds you that the public good takes second place; I pray that that Lord who died in Jerusalem may find a cure and make you ashamed, so that – some day – reason may constrain you into retaining your good name.]

The poem is set in the old town of Edinburgh. In Dunbar's day, its boundaries stretched along the narrow ridge from the Castle in the west to Holyrood in the east. The northern extremity was marked by the North Loch, where Princes Street Gardens and Waverley Station now stand. To the south, where the Meadows are sited, stood the South Loch and the Burgh Muir. Two miles away was the busy port of Leith.

In setting and topic, 'To the Merchantis' is not a courtly poem. It looks beyond Holyroodhouse, recently built by James, moving up the Royal Mile to the area around St Giles (your parish kirk: 3:2)^2, where the business life of Edinburgh was conducted. The viewpoint it presents is a courtly one, however. Whether Dunbar was commissioned by James IV or not, he is certainly telling the merchant burghers of Edinburgh that the king has advanced their status and now expects them to repay this by thinking of the social good. The opening lines of the final stanza put the case most directly. Monetary profit and social service must now march together (11:1–2).

How is the argument developed? In Stanza 1, the merchants' self-serving conservatism is implicitly contrasted with the king's more liberal thinking (1:2–3). Recent domestic reforms had delegated greater power to the merchants and the town council. This administrative change is reflected in Dunbar's constant references to Edinburgh as 'your' town (1:2; 2:1; 3:1 etc). If it is their town, however, the merchants' reputation and the town's become interrelated (1:4). The concomitant of this is that James may withdraw those privileges he has himself gifted. Another region, it is suggested, stands in the wings should it be necessary to move royal favour and the institutions of government elsewhere (1:6–7).

Stanzas 2 and 3 present, in one vivid cameo, a major problem facing James IV. While Holyrood was a centre of culture and comfort, fit to impress European dignitaries, Scotland was still a comparatively poor and barbarous country. In Edinburgh, any visiting dignitary who left the palace to move up the Royal Mile would be forced into the centre of a dark street piled high with the middens on to which fishmongers and butchers threw their trimmings (2:1–2). The angry jostlings and the bad-tempered arguments were in part due to this (2:3–4). Everyone wanted to keep in the safer, cleaner centre of the road. Scotland's practically unique architecture intensified the problem as the outside stairs of the houses also impinged on the narrow thoroughfare (3:2–3).

Stanzas 4 and 6 distinguish the superior position of the merchants from that of craftsmen. Shrewdly, Dunbar says just what the first group want to hear. The merchants had shops, lived in Edinburgh, paid for its upkeep and dealt in luxury items ('gold and silk'). The craftsmen came in from the suburbs, bringing portable stalls with them; they did not pay town taxes and dealt in common commodities ('crudis and milk'; 'pansches, pudingis'). Stanza 4 shows how the lowlier group are setting out their wares in front of the merchants' premises (4:1–4). Self-interest and the common good converge in demanding a change of practice. Stanza 6 narrows the focus and adopts a more bitter tone. Tailors, cobblers and other low artisans vie incongruously with the dignified trade of the merchants in the cramped, dark honeycomb of the capital's business district (6:1–4).

The case dearest to Dunbar's own heart is set as a parenthesis

(Stanza 5) within these two stanzas. The rising middle class tried to mimic royal practice by hiring minstrels. Foreseeably, the leading 'makar' in the land views their choice and tastes with disdain. If these merchants really wish to attain a good name for themselves, they should appoint skilled wordsmiths like himself, not mad barkers at the moon whose repertory is limited to the simplest of folk songs (5:1–7).

Stanzas 7 and 8 are concerned with the immediate effects of a recent outbreak of the plague in Scotland. Disease on a large scale, then as now, draws the maimed into the major centres of population. Entries in the Edinburgh Town Council Records of the 1520s would later confirm Dunbar's definition of the two prevalent lines of thought on this continuing social problem. Some councillors wanted to send home *all* those vagabonds ('*Any maner* of vagaboundis') who were to be found begging piteously by the wayside. The more humane approach advocated by Dunbar did win the day. If it proved practicable, care should be offered only to genuine cases, while those who feigned illness but actually were 'stark (strong) and may wirk (work)' ought to be deported. Dunbar's earlier description of Edinburgh as a beggars' nest where honest folk can get no peace (7:1–4) explains the root and branch view but only as a prelude to criticising the merchants' selfish pursuit of it (7:5–7; 8:5–7).

He humanely contrasts their wealth with the poverty of the genuinely disadvantaged (8:1–2) but sets that emotive, idealistic argument between two more businesslike warnings. James IV had recently reformed the law, making it easier for the poor to appeal (9:1–3). If the merchants do not continue these reforms, the king may well be tempted to renege on his decision to centre these improvements in Edinburgh.

More personally and more pertinently, the merchants should not confuse short term with long term self-interest (8:1–7). This theme has run throughout the poem, emphasised by the refrain's repetitive emphasis on their good name. If this general opposition is summed up generally in Stanza 8, the next two stanzas refer it specifically to Edinburgh and its merchants. James is relying on them to give practical support to his farsighted policies (9:1–5). If they do not, then the 'uther regioun', referred to in Stanza 1, will be anxious to take over (9:6–7).

Stanza 10's set of advisory guidelines are not just the warblings of some unimportant versifier. They are voiced by a paid servant of the king with the force of that decisive monarch behind him. Nor does Dunbar confine himself to positive suggestions for fair practice. The identity of the rival town which may supplant Edinburgh becomes threateningly clearer. Royal Burgh charters of the day permitted the small group of merchants concerned with, say, gold to agree on an artificially high price for that commodity. Monopolies and the extortions emanating from them (10:4) were not permitted in Baronial Burghs. The major burgh of that type was Stirling. The king had a palace in that town; it was centrally based and its merchants were quite highly regarded.

Stanza 11 provides the highest, divine context. That there are different ways of looking at the issue, Dunbar does not deny. The merchants may continue in their belief that short term self-interest is the best policy. Alternatively, customer confidence might be served through prioritising the common good.

The loving, sacrificial example of Christ is drawn in at this point to shame the merchants into the latter course (11:3–5). Even at this highest level, Dunbar remembers whom he is addressing. He knows better than to conclude an address to businessmen on too idealistic a note. 'Common proffeit' may be the best way theologically, as well as sociologically, morally, politically and practically, but it could also maximise long term profit.

Dunbar's appeal to the merchants is founded on practical considerations. As it is written in a form of Middle Scots close to the conversational norm, it may serve another pragmatic purpose – that of bridging the language gap. Study of a single poem may not introduce the student to the full riches of Middle Scots but it can define the major areas of difficulty and suggest some helpful strategies for dealing with them.

Early writers, it was noted, thought of their 'endyting' (composition; writing) aurally, as the imaginative branch of speechmaking. Dunbar usually describes his verse as 'sangis' (songs) or 'ballattis' (ballads); works to be sung or recited aloud. Most students do find that an attempt to read Middle Scots texts aloud, without concern for changes in pronunciation, makes it seem less strange than when they simply view it on the page. As Dunbar is a poet with an especially fine ear for the rhythms and modulations of spoken Scots, the technique works very well in his case. The ear will catch and the voice adapt to the phrasing and sense he desires, even when the reader is coming fresh to the older tongue.

Those who are acquainted with modern Scots dialects will, inevitably, have some advantages. Stanza 3, line 2 illustrates the two areas in which this benefit principally resides. A Scots voice is able to sound the Germanic 'ch' sound in 'lycht'. Anyone versed in modern Scots will translate 'kirk' as 'church' with no need of a glossary. In practice, students without these advantages do not feel disadvantaged for long.

The appearance of the text on the page sets up the first set of 'strangenesses'. The most obvious difference from modern spelling is the presence of a new symbol – 'ȝ'. In the opening line, for example, 'ȝe merchantis' are addressed. 'ȝ' is yogh, a letter shared with Middle English. In the phrase 'ȝe merchantis', it represents the voiced sound 'y' in 'ye' (you). But it may also signify unvoiced 'hh' as in the 'Tailȝouris' (Tailors) of 6:1. The shape of the letter led printers erroneously to substitute 'z' for 'ȝ' rather than 'y'. 'ȝe merchantis' means 'You ('Ye') merchantis'. This is why Culzean is written with 'z' but pronounced with voiceless 'hh'.

Prior to printing, spelling systems were largely unstandardised. Scots writers may use the 'ch' sound in the Middle Scots word for 'neighbours', while the 'gh' form was preferred in Middle English. Yet, in 10:6, the form 'nighbouris' is used by a poet who elsewhere writes 'nichtbour', 'nychtburis' and 'nychtbouris'. Another variant is 'sklander', spelt with a 'k' in 3:7 only for 'sclander' to be favoured in the next two refrains (4:7; 5:7).

The main letters affected by the looseness of spelling conventions are 'u', 'v' and 'w'; 'i' and 'j'; 'f' and 'ff'. Dunbar seldom uses those forms which look really peculiar and were more regularly favoured in Early Scots. In 5:3, he prefers 'nevir' to 'newir' or 'neuir', although 'w' or 'u' might then represent consonantal 'v' orthographically. The word 'uther' in the same line is, fairly obviously, Middle Scots for 'other'. The alternative forms, 'vther' or 'wther', might cause more trouble but are avoided. Nor does Dunbar normally use 'i' for consonantal 'j'. He has 'Jok and James', not 'Iok and Iames' in 4:4. 5:2 has 'Joun' rather than 'Ioun' and 11:4 prefers 'Jerusalem' to 'Ierusalem'. On the other hand, occasional use of 'ff' for 'f' is a feature of his writing, as in 'ȝourselff' (6:7).

The vowels 'i' and 'y' were also interchangeable. No Middle Scots poet would accuse another of misspelling 'fine' as 'fyne'. Either would be possible. Dunbar does tend to prefer 'i' for the short vowel form, as in modern 'hit', and either 'y' or 'ie'[3] for the longer diphthong in modern 'sigh'. So, in 3:1 and 6:3 he has 'stinkand styll' and 'hie' in 4.1. 'Think' is preferred to 'Thynk' in the refrain line while 'fynd' appears rather than 'find' in 11:3.

The good news is that most editors will use the variant form closest to modern practice.[4] This is the principle followed elsewhere in this book. It is well to know the full situation, however, so that you are ready to test out the effect of the sounds 'y' or 'hh' when a Middle Scots text shows 'ȝ' or to substitute consonantal 'v' when trying to understand odd forms in 'w' or 'u'.

The other main problems may be covered by a second, this time linguistic, journey through the text. Stanza 1, for example, has the Scots form 'quh' for 'wh' in 'Quhy' (1:1). 'Quhat' and 'quhilk' are the Scots equivalent of 'what' and 'which' in Middle and Modern English. It should also be noted that the characteristic Scots plural noun form in 'is' does not normally have syllabic force, so 'merchantis' (1:1) has two syllables rather than three. The rhyme scheme in Stanza 2 – 'gaittis', 'scaittis', 'debaittis' and 'estaittis' – should, accordingly, be read with the same syllabic values as in Modern English. The alternative '-es' and '-is' spelling forms appear in the 'panches and pudingis' variation of 4:4.

Stanza 3 exhibits an important difference affecting the verb. The present participle in Middle Scots usually ends in '-and'. The alleyway in 3:1 and 6:3 is described as 'stinkand' rather than 'stinking', the normal form in Chaucerean English. As it was Chaucer's south-eastern dialect which became the major source of Modern English, it is generally closer than Middle Scots to our reading expectations. Stanzas 3 and 4, for example, mirror the retention of the 'k' sound and spelling in 'kirk' and 'ilk', when sound changes in southern Middle English had already established the 'ch' sound in modern 'church and 'each'. But Stanza 3 also proves that exceptions to this rule exist. Middle Scots favours the modern '-s' ending for the third person singular, present tense of the verb; Middle English still preferred '-eth'. The alleyway, accordingly, 'standis' rather than 'standeth' in 3:1.

The transposition of sounds, known as metathesis, is exemplified in 4:2 where 'crudis' anticipates modern 'curdis'. The Scots form of the past participle – 'hamperit' rather than 'hampered' – may be seen in 6:4. In Stanza 8, the forms 'proffeit...dois incres' (8:1) and 'ye...dois posses' (8:6) illustrate another troublesome fact. In Middle Scots the 's' form exists in the present tense, not only where modern practice would lead us to expect it – 'Profit does increase' but unexpectedly, in the second and third person plural forms as well 'You (merchants) does possess'. The addition of 'dois' here, as in 6:2 and 11:1, was an alternative way of rendering the simple present. A literal translation would read 'profit increases' and 'you possess'. Dunbar is not clumsily introducing 'dois' in order to eke out the metre.

Finally, there are advantages and disadvantages in facing a language which is not so distinct from English as is French or German. 'Sen' in 9:1 and 'gif' in 9:6 belong to the first category. They look odd but require no Einstein to deduce that they mean 'since' and 'if' respectively. On the negative side, there are words whose apparent closeness to modern forms is deceptive. In 5:1 'tone' means 'tune' while in 2:6, 'estaittis' has the social sense of 'ranks'. Different associative ranges also exist. 'Godlie' in 8:2 suggests at once godly and good.

Having discussed social history and language, it is now time to consider the literary conventions of the day. From now on, only the most difficult quotations will be translated in full.

Notes
1. The letter 'ȝ' is discussed fully on page 19. It may be voiceless, having much the same force as a glottal stop – the 'z' in Culzean represents the yogh sound. When voiced, as here, it is pronounced like the 'y' in 'you' or 'yesterday'.
2. References to texts will either cite stanza and line number within stanza as here (3:2 = line two in stanza three) or the line number simply (16) depending on ease of application.
3. In Middle Scots an added 'e', as in 'schame' was usually not sounded but indicated that the preceding vowel was long.
4. MacKay MacKenzie does follow most of these procedures. His policy of normalising 'u', 'v' and 'w' only when they resolve what seem *to him* ambiguities, however, make the advice given above relevant even for those using his text.

CHAPTER THREE

The Ladder of Style: Devilishness, Death and Divinity

Today, most people are literate. Publishers, influenced by profit margins, pour out a variety of literary forms for huge popular audiences. Realism, prose and the novel are, foreseeably, favoured because they are the easiest to adapt to. In the late fifteenth century, the aims of art and the conditions under which imaginative composition was undertaken were very different. Manuscript transmission and widespread illiteracy meant small audiences and reading aloud. Literature justified itself in educational terms, with poetry by far the dominant mode. It was viewed as a craft with its own rules; these were distinct from life and needed to be laboured at by writer and audience alike.

Dunbar's older contemporary, Robert Henryson, in the 'Prologue' to his collection of moral fables, uses a sporting image to explain the three major aims of the makar. Sport, like verse, involves *working* at skills. It aims, nonetheless, to provide *relaxation.* He employs an image from archery to underline this point. If one always stretches out the bowstring of life seriously, it will break. Poetry, therefore, uses 'terms... which are pleasing to men's ears'.

It is the third criterion which is of most importance at this stage. A game involves *specific rules* which may themselves alter, depending on the code chosen. Picking up the ball may be a good idea in rugby but not in football. These rules operate according to a logic which differs markedly from that governing real life. A ball rolling down High Street does not warrant your picking it up, handing off some passers-by and touching down at the traffic lights.

Inevitably, art of this sort will have minority appeal because it implies mastering the craft of art as well as that of life. The Victorian Realist movement was the first chronologically to make a virtue out of direct presentation of lived reality. Today, many television viewers are so seduced by the method in its soap opera form that they write giving practical advice to the imagined characters of the soap operas on how to lead their 'real' lives. By stressing the distance between the categories of language and of nature, between the patterned structures of art and the flux of life, earlier writers avoid this problem. But they do so at the cost of losing those of their audience who are innocent about art; those who look at a painting labelled 'Horse', with only the criterion of a real horse in mind. Picasso and Henryson will usually frustrate that simple expectation. Dunbar, with his personal, down to earth vision will only do so sometimes. The task of Chapters Three and Four is to define when, and in what ways, he plays laboriously.

To start with style is, in his case, inevitable, for he is, above all, a lover of words. Classical writers taught that an author should mirror the dignity or otherwise of the topic and/or person addressed through the form of language used. Reduced to its simplest, medieval form, this principle of Decorum set down guidelines for three major styles and their related themes. The high or aureate style was complex and expansive; it drew its vocabulary mainly from Latin and French and was thought appropriate for praising gods, kings and nobles. The normal or middle style, already exemplified in 'To the Merchantis', was the closest to ordinary speech; it was thought suitable for the middle classes and undramatic arguments. The low style was usually reserved for vituperation, farce and the lower classes; it had a characteristically staccato rhythm, often pointed by alliteration, and drew many of its loanwords from Dutch and Norse.

It is the artistry of these styles which first strikes a reader of Dunbar. The attack on courtiers in 'Remonstrance to the King' may simply be a list – but the words and rhythms have been very carefully chosen and conform to the guidelines governing the Low Style:

Fenyeouris°, fleichouris° and flatteraris,	pretenders; cajolers
Cryaris, craikaris°, and clatteraris°;	bickerers; chatterers
Soukaris°, groukaris, gledaris°, gunnaris;	parasites; bloodsuckers
Monsouris° of France, gud clarat-cunnaris°...	Monsoors; connisoors

(p. 37, lines 39–42)

Dunbar is not trying to imitate accurately the insults of the street but labouring to re-present them skilfully within the codes of the flyting tradition. The sustained alliteration on only two rhyming sounds broadcasts this craftsmanship.

In formal flyting competitions at court, two poets would insult each other in verse. Their audience would then judge which of them had won the contest. This was a poetic game with victory going to the more skilful exponent of the form. It did not imply that one poet actually despised his opponent. But, of course, the aggressive techniques of that game could also be used in satiric verse. When Dunbar attacks the courtiers in 'Remonstrance to the King', those sections of the piece, which use the sustained invective of flyting, *are* seriously and malevolently intended. I have chosen to concentrate on three of Dunbar's finest works, each of which will represent one of the major stylistic registers. His venomous satire against 'The Fenyeit Freir (Friar) of Tungland' (p. 67) stands on the lower rungs and begins the ascent.

The story behind this poem is related by the sixteenth-century Scottish historian, Bishop Leslie:

> This tyme ther wes ane Italiane with the King, quha wes maid Abbott of Tungland and wes of curious ingyne (had an inquisitive turn of mind) ... This Abbot tuik in hand to flie with wingis, and to be in Fraunce befoir the saidis... ambassadours; and to that effect (to achieve this) he causet mak ane pair of wingis of fedderis, quhilks beand fessinit apoun him, he flew of the castell wall of Striveling (Stirling) and brak his thee bane (thigh bone); bot the wyt (blame) thairof he asscryvit to that (the blame for this he ascribed to the fact that) thair was sum hen fedderis in the wingis, quhilk yarnit (yearned for) ... the middyng (midden) and not the skyis.[1]

One might take a reasonably favourable view of this first recorded Scottish attempt at flying. The Italian must have believed in his experiment or he would not have sought a competition with the ambassadors, which involved leaping off the battlements of Stirling Castle as they, more safely, rode out below. He has also something of Falstaff's resilience. Instead of accepting that his scheme was foolish he will go back to the drawing board and begin again, avoiding the feathers of birds which do not fly.

His proclaimed trade of alchemy might also have been benevolently interpreted. Essentially, it attempted to turn base metals into gold by processes of heating and purifying. Some writers saw these activities, and the rituals associated with providing a quintessence which would unite and transcend the four known elements, as a shadow of God's mysterious means and purposes for mankind. The alternative view is that it represents a devilish short cut to knowledge through magic.

Dunbar leaves his listeners in little doubt about his view of Abbot Damian's unfortunate flight. The form he chooses is that of the dream vision. The opening five lines announce that the poet has fallen asleep and is dreaming. The events described are, therefore, an inventive recalling of the events at Stirling. Formally, they are in the middle of two brief waking moments. Noises within the dream do not awaken the narrator – 'I walknit with the noyis' – until four lines from the end (line 125).

Dream vision poetry is usually associated with the high style and noble characters. While Dunbar initially seems to confirm that form and style by referring grandiosely to Aurora and the orient

(1–2), the effect is short-lived. After all, even the high-sounding invocation of the dawn is proposed in 'cuttit vers' or 'rime couée'. This heavily rhymed stanza with its short and heavily emphasised rhythms needs careful handling to avoid becoming doggerel.[2] As such it was often used for low style parodies of pretentiousness. That is the purpose to which Dunbar turns it.

In what ways does his invention transform the historical facts? The satiric vision begins with personal animosity. To Dunbar, as revealed in Chapter One, this foreigner, pseudo-scientist and pseudo-priest, must have encapsulated all the things he most detested. To add insult to injury, he had gained the benefice which Dunbar so evidently coveted.

All his scientific trades are maliciously presented. As false chemist, he caused pain (29); as a doctor, he murdered his patients (30); as leech, he only asked for the skin of his victim and a horse as attendance fees (33–35). As alchemist, his frequent attempts to provide James IV with the quintessence had failed (58–9).

When Dunbar wrote, poetry clearly distinguished its means and aims from the rival disciplines of history and philosophy. They used reason to account for facts and ideas respectively; poetry used imagination to test *both* facts *and* ideas within the realm of potentiality. In taking all of the alchemist's weaknesses to their farthest possible extremes, he can at once fulfil the defined remit of his craft and satisfy all the personal frustrations felt by one Scottish artist, confronted by kingly favouritism for foreigners and science.

Damian's pretensions to piety evoke an equally bitter but differently slanted imagistic rejoinder. His Italian birth and journey via France to Scotland is introduced via a fanciful Mohammedan odyssey. As a Turk from Tartary he enters the land of the Saracens ('Barbary' 6) before claiming a home in Lombardy (5–7). This unbaptised abbot (9–11), who never attends mass (49), may be meant to purify the souls of his flock; in fact he only evacuates their bowels (44). His Satanic descent is noted (4) while he is associated with the devil's servants, the giants (32), and vies with the devil in guile ('dissimulance' 13).

Human flight is also an attempt to move into the divine realms of the air and, as such, an act of pride. This was held to be the definitive sin of Satan, so dream logic turns the leap from Stirling Castle into a miniature re-enactment of Satan's rebellion against God. Damian's duplicity having been discovered, he decides to return to Turkey by air (57–61). Stealing feathers from a variety of birds, he rises to unnatural heights but they attack him and take back their plumage.

Not only the abbot reaches the heights at this point, Dunbar's powers of expression also scale new heights of intensity:

Thik was a clud° of kayis° and crawis,	cloud; jackdaws
Of marleyonis°, mittanis°, and of mawis°,	merlins; birds of prey; gulls
That bikkrit° at his berd° with blawis	attacked; beard
In battell him abowt.	
Thay nybbillit him with noyis and cry,	
The rerd° of thame rais° to the sky,	noise; rose
And evir he cryit on Fortoun, 'Fy!'	
His lyfe° was in to dowt°.	continued existence; doubt

(p. 69, lines 89–95)

The eight syllable/six syllable pattern of *rime couée*, designed for rapid movement, is intensified by internal rhyme and heavy alliteration. Dunbar's visualising powers are also at their acutest. Earlier, he had hung a kestrel in each of Damian's ears ('A stanchell hang in ilka lug' 82). Now all the birds grab their feathers back. As the aviator-alchemist comes to earth, the narrator enthusiastically consigns him 'up to the ene (eyes)' (107) in a fetid pool. He lies there for three days, while around him the sky darkens as the cloud of birds screams its triumph:

Thre dayis in dub° amang the dukis°	stagnant pool; ducks
He did with dirt him hyde.	
The air was dirkit with the fowlis°,	birds
That come with yawmeris° and with yowlis…°	yells; howls

(p. 70, lines 119–22)

But this literally dark form of comedy has an even deadlier allegorical application.

The hilarious details which Dunbar uses to mock the abbot also re-enact paradoxically the events of the crucifixion. At Christ's passing the skies had darkened as well; he too sank beneath the earth into the nether world for three days before rising. The feigned friar replays in filthy, Satanic fashion that portion of the Christian story in which the devil is defeated for ever. Immersion up to the eyes confirms that this pseudo-scientist does so as an unregenerate benighted follower of evil.

In using a specific event to satirise life at the court of James IV, Dunbar is following the aesthetic guidelines of his day. Teachers of rhetoric urged that the literal story line should be enjoyed for itself but also employed to teach lessons relevant to other branches of knowledge. In this case, the feigned friar becomes a vehicle for attacking political policies, hypocritical morals and the theology of the anti-Christ. These, in his opinion, should fall with the ludicrous prelate into the pool of ignominy.

In high or low styles, Dunbar has no problem in displaying his verbal skills. Both are overtly rhetorical styles in the modern sense of that word. Rhetoric, however, provided guidelines for *all* styles, including the one which came closest to the words and rhythms of everyday speech. In 'Lament for the Makaris' he uses this middle style to provide two lists. First, there are the classes of people who have fallen victim to death and then there are individual poets, who have taken the same route.

The second list begins in Stanza 13 with Chaucer:

He° hes done petuously° devour,	i.e. Death; piteously
The noble Chaucer, of makaris flour°,	flower among poets
The monk of Bery°, and Gower, all thre°;	Lydgate; three
Timor mortis conturbat me.	*The fear of death disturbs me*

(p. 21, lines 49–52)

This seems about as dramatic as versifying the telephone book. Yet, when Richard Burton was asked to read his three favourite poems, the 'Lament' was one of those chosen. How does Dunbar, when imitating the conversational middle style, make a series of types and names dramatic?

In answering this, I shall take up the earlier suggestion that reading aloud may prove a helpful way of coming to terms with the language. Linguistically, the middle style is the easiest to understand. Nonetheless, three additional characteristics of Middle Scots may be deduced from this rollcall of death:

(i) The first line, 'I that in heill wes and gladnes' ('I, who was in a state of health and gladness) demonstrates Middle Scots use of 'that' as a relative pronoun. This grammatical feature becomes more of a barrier to understanding, when the reduced form 'at' or the Scots form 'quhilk' and 'quhilkis' are substituted.
(ii) 'Hes done...devour' (l.49) simply means 'devoured'. Middle Scots often forms the past (preterite) in this way. 'Can' or 'gar' plus the infinitive are alternatives – 'can devour', 'gar devour'.
(iii) Misleadingly 'easy' phrases are, if anything, more common in this style than the low or high. 'For the deid' (l.96) may look like 'for the dead ones' or, perhaps, 'for the deed' but actually conveys, 'For death (itself)'. In line 61, given the poem's topic,

'berevit' seems certain to mean 'bereaved' but actually retains the older sense of 'taken away'.

With meaning clarified, Burton's discovery of drama in lists may be pursued. There is a sense in which monotonous repetition underlines death's relentless march and so itself becomes a dramatic effect. The dignified Latin refrain marks out its inevitability like a funeral drumbeat. *'Timor mortis conturbat me'* was part of the intoned services of the church. Congregations were invited by the priest to chant these words as the seventh response in the third nocturn of the Office of the Dead. Its associations are emotively powerful.

The speaking voice is encouraged through syntactic repetition to build up a sense of melancholy. Dunbar personifies Death and uses repetition of the 'he' plus 'verb' form stylistically to embody the fact that no one escapes the grim reaper. 'He takis' (21, 29), 'He sparis' (33), 'He hes done...devour' (49), 'he hes tane' (55), 'he hes berevit' (61), 'he nocht...levit' (62), 'he hes tane' (65), 'He hes...slaine' (69–70), 'He hes reft' (73), 'He hes tane' (77), 'he hes done roune' (81), 'he hes...tane' (85, 93).

Subtle verbal and syntactic variations do exist. These often mark off structural divisions. The present tense changes to the past in Stanza 13, when specific poets enter the drama for the first time. At the end of that movement, the transition from past to present is underlined by the echoing of Stanza 20's 'he hes tane' in Stanza 22 but with the phrase 'last of aw' added. Similarity highlights difference.

One is guided, nonetheless, towards a measured reading of the text. Out of the 25 stanzas, the two lists take up 19. Far from solving the initial problem of incipient monotony, this appears to intensify it. Where is the drama which Burton sensed, and how is it conveyed?

The poem's sub-title, 'Quhen he wes sek (sick)', provides the first clue. Like Shakespearean spirits, these ghosts are called up by a troubled soul. The first stanza makes that clear:

I that in heill° wes and gladnes,	health
Am trublit now with gret° seiknes°,	severe; sickness
And feblit with infermite°;	weakened by infirmity
Timor mortis conturbat me.	

(p. 20, lines 1–4)

A bout of illness has made Dunbar[3] think seriously about life. I do not believe the poem encourages a reader to transmit despair or panic. When reading it aloud, I try to put myself in the character of a downcast, reflective man, suddenly made aware that he too must die some time. Certainly, Burton used an understated, slow delivery, only speeding up or becoming passionate in obedience to Dunbar's stylistic promptings.

What are these promptings? If one thinks of the film technique of panning in and out, Dunbar begins with a close, personal focus – '*I* that in heill wes' (1), then pans gradually outwards. '*Our* plesance' (5) embraces his immediate audience. A wider lens is used in Stanzas 3 and 4. Not only those who listen to him but all people in all time, everywhere, fall to death – 'The stait of *man* dois change and vary' (9), 'No stait *in erd* (on earth) heir standis sickir (safe)' (13).

The syntax throughout the introductory portion remains simple. Only the Latin refrain suggests a movement towards the high style as this is a vision of mystery viewed from earth. Yet slightly more complex forms are introduced as tension builds up. The third line of Stanza 2 has two short clauses, the second in Stanza 3 breaks into four. While this gently accelerates the voice, the final stanza in the group, with its parenthetic image, 'As with the wynd wavis the wickir' (14), slows down delivery once more. The first piece of overt craftsmanship, the rhythmically evocative echoing of the word 'wavis' in Stanza 4, marks the transition from philosophy to pageant.

Stanzas 5 to 23 contain the two lists. Dunbar reverses the visual procedure of the opening, starting with the broadest focus and panning in. Stanzas 5–11 deal with 'all Estatis' (ranks) in the land. They are introduced through a set of contrasts. Knights on the field are followed by babies at their mothers' breasts; imprisoned men abroad give way to ladies, imprisoned in another sense, at home. This pageant is, more accurately, a varied series of images passing through a perturbed mind. Unsurprisingly, self-interest soon narrows the perspective. From types in the world at large, the poet shifts to those men of learning ('Na clerk' 34) who share his own interests. The sub-divisions of learning are then enumerated in Stanzas 10 and 11, leaving Stanza 12 to introduce the actual lament for the makaris (poets):

I se that makaris° amang the laif°	poets; rest
Playis heir ther pageant, syne° gois to graif°;	then; grave
Sparit is nocht ther faculte°;	faculty
Timor mortis conturbat me.	

(p. 21, 45–8)

Dunbar does not think of Scots and English poets as belonging to separate nationalist camps. He regularly confesses his admiration for the leaders of that pageant, Chaucer, Lydgate and Gower. The procession which follows, however, is a specifically Scottish one. While Dunbar does not follow a strict chronology, the ghostly movement does draw ever closer to his own day. Only when he reaches his contemporaries do emotive words and images obtrude. The long dead Barbour and Clerk of Tranent have simply been 'taken', Gilbert Hay has been 'ended'. These are bald statements, Henryson's more recent death, on the other hand, warrants elaboration. The Dunfermline poet heard death whisper in his ear while John Ross has been embraced by it. Dark Biblical associations, with Satan in the garden of Eden and Judas in the garden of Gethsemane respectively, are encouraged.

Only the 'last [victims] of aw', in Stanzas 22 and 23, evoke pathos directly. Dunbar joins in the universal sense of compassion felt at the loss of Quentin Shaw. Should Walter Kennedy, currently on his death-bed, be taken as well, that event will arouse great pity ('gret reuth'). Traditionally, such thoughts of love and mercy lead into a joyous Christian conclusion.

Dunbar's verses on life as pilgrimage witness to his belief in this final triumph, but the 'Lament' concludes in faith without joy. A tone of thoughtful regret opens and ends the poem. I have highlighted the words I would accentuate and marked the short (/) and long (//) pauses I would take in reading the final stanzas.

Sen° he has all my brether° tane, /   Since; brothers
He will nocht lat **me** lif **alane**°, //   be alive uniquely
On forse° / I man° his nyxt pray° be;   Perforce; must; prey
*Timor mortis conturbat **me**.*

Sen for the deid° / remeid° is none, //   death; remedy
Best is / that **we** for dede **dispone**°,   dispose ourselves
Eftir our deid / that lif may we; //
*Timor mortis conturbat **me**.*
                (p.22, lines 93–100)

Any reading is in part a personal interpretation. I would take these stanzas slowly to emphasise the return to personal misery, mirrored in the poem's structure. Reflective stanzas (1–4; 24–25) frame the two lists (5–12; 13–23). The highlighting of Latin *me*, in reading the refrain, is intended to remind the listener that every stanza has ended with the poet referring to himself – 'The fear of death worries **me**'. Rather than escaping eagerly from the closure of this formal circle into the transcendental arms of God, Dunbar uses 'on forse', 'remeid is none' and 'best...for dede dispone' to suggest an unwilling, if stoical, acceptance of death. Paradoxically, a poet who constantly moans about this world's unfairness, appears to cling lovingly to its pleasures.

This is to release the latent drama within the lament, not to impose intensity upon recalcitrant material. To those who cannot see beyond monotonous listing effects, another list of proper critical objections has been offered. The repetition of one name after another has a cumulative dramatic effect suited to contemplation of death's inevitability. The problem is one of degree. Monotony is a proper part of the poem but must not define it entirely.

Changes of focus, syntax and tone guarantee that this will not happen, as do the theatrical pageant motif and the personification of the major villain. The narrator's formal ordering of his material guides readers towards these subtleties as does his handling of the middle style. Movements within and, occasionally, away from the register provide the carefully modulated linguistic foundation for this gently ominous drama of death. What appears simply boring is, in fact, 'made' powerful by understated skills.

The vast chasm between middle style understatement and the self-advertisement of the high style may be conveyed economically. With the quatrains of the 'Lament' in mind, look at the following stanzas:

Ane Ballat of Our Lady

Hale, sterne superne°! hale in eterne°,	star heavenly; eternity
In Godis sicht to schyne!	
Lucerne in derne° for to discerne	lantern in darkness
Be glory and grace devyne;	
5 Hodiern, modern, sempitern°,	to-day, now, for ever
Angelicall regyne°!	queen
Our tern inferne° for to dispern°	infernal gloom; dispel
Helpe, rialest rosyne°.	most royal rose
Ave Maria, gracia plena°!	Hail Mary, full of grace
10 Haile, fresche floure femynyne!	
Yerne° us, guberne°, virgin matern°,	diligently govern us; maternal
Of reuth° baith rute° and ryne°.	pity; root; bark
Haile, yhyng°, benyng°, fresche flurising!	young; gracious
Haile, Alphais habitakle°!	Alpha's habitation
15 Thy dyng° ofspring maid us to syng	worthy
Befor his tabernakle°;	tabernacle
All thing maling° we doune thring°	malign; thrust
Be sicht of his signakle°;	symbol (cross)
Quhilk king us bring unto his ryng°,	reign/ring

20 Fro dethis dirk umbrakle°.	dark shade
Ave Maria gracia plena!	*Hail, Mary, full of grace*
Haile, moder and maide but makle!	spotless
Bricht syng°, gladyng our languissing°	sign, languishing
Be micht° of thi mirakle°.	power; your miracle[4]

(pp. 160–1, lines 1–24)

Anyone who expects art to mirror life is going to find this at best puzzling, at worst impenetrable.

First, there is the diction. This is certainly not the language of conversation. No medieval Scot in his right mind would hail a lady in the street as 'fresche floure femynyne'. This is the consciously poetic language of the aureate style, suited to Christ's mother because of her closeness to God. In terms of 'making', she warrants a verse-cathedral. By using complex vocabulary drawn mainly from Latin (e.g. 'hodiern', 'sempitern', 'umbrakle') and French (e.g. 'habitakle', 'maling', 'languissing') Dunbar consciously distances his art in its artificiality from the expectations of the real world. Aesthetics and decorum determine the rules for this work, not the behaviour of one's neighbours.

People do not naturally speak in verse but in prose. Dunbar and his contemporaries employ verse as the most basic sign that their world is one of artifice. In inviting us to listen to their songs and ballads, they self-consciously invite us into a different world – a world of skilful word-crafting in which they are the qualified master-builders. High style verse for the Virgin had, of course, to be the most obviously elaborate of all and so the stanza form chosen for 'Ane Ballat' is ambitious in the extreme. It has five lines with triple rhyme on one sound twining around six lines all rhyming on another. In Stanza 1, lines 1, 3, 5, 7 and 11 produce fifteen rhymes on 'ern(e)'; lines 2, 4, 6, 8, 10 and 12 have six rhymes on 'yne'. The Latin quotation from St Luke 1.28 and 1.42 stands unchanged at line 9 throughout the piece. This pattern of twenty-one rhymes on two sounds is sustained throughout the seven stanzas of the poem.

To be contrived implies being unnatural, but unnatural contrivance is the highest aim of late medieval rhetorical theory. Unsurprisingly, therefore, the story-line on which most popular writing relies is practically non-existent. Indeed, a not inaccurate précis of the hymn's eighty-four lines might read, 'Praise, more praise and even more praise be to Mary'. As imagination is the distinctive faculty of the poet and the high style represents the purest verse of all, visual images rather than 'Once upon a time' dictate the sequence of ideas within the poem. In Stanzas 1 and 2 alone, Mary is compared to lights (star and lantern); to earthly and spiritual rulers (queen...most royal; the king's mother); to plants (rose; tree) and to protective receptacles (habitation; tabernacle).

Study of the sources for these image lines and their ordering within the poem draws us deeper into artifice. If Dunbar uses the high style to imitate images rather than life, these images turn out to be, themselves, artificial. The four classes of imagery defined above are drawn from four different traditions in painting and sculpture.

Mary as the star imitates those paintings which show her wearing a star on the shoulder of her cloak or on her breast. This was usually blue, for the symbol derived from her Jewish name, Miriam – *stella maris* – star of the sea. This is the Mary of Advent, as Dunbar's later reference to her as the day-star will confirm.

Although the regal Virgin was more often a subject of sculpture than drawing, frescoes in medieval churches often showed her enthroned. In this tradition, which emphasised her power and wisdom, she normally carried an orb and wore a crown. Christ was seldom present because, allegorically, she symbolised the early Church. Any companions, therefore, are smaller mortals, reliant on her and the institution she represents as intermediaries on their behalf.

Mary as flowering plant derives from mystic and penitential lines of thought. The rose suggested both the red of martyrdom and the white of purity. When that rose is placed in paradise or in an enclosed garden the *Song of Solomon*, literally, enters the picture. St Bernard and other initiators of the cult of Mary interpreted the lyrics of the lover and his bride allegorically. According to them, they foreshadowed many of the miracles associated with the Virgin. Thornless rose, rose bower and garden all signified the virgin birth; Dunbar evokes every one of these images in 'Ane Ballat' before explicitly referring to the 'ros virginall' in his last stanza.

The protective Mary imagined as tabernacle, temple or hospice had a similar allegorical force. Visually, all three suggest the womb which contained divinity just as convincingly as the rose bower or enclosed garden. But it is the Virgin's merciful and maternal aspects which are highlighted in paintings and sculptures using this symbolism.

These image lines interlock in a way which confirms the techniques used for versification. Analogies of light, regality, plants and refuge repeat, vary and intertwine just as the rhyme scheme does. For example, Mary as star will overtly be recalled in Stanzas 3, 5, 6, and more suggestively referred to in Stanza 7. In each case there is a slight variation. The supernal star (1) becomes in turn the oriental star (3), the day-star (54) and the mediterranean star (70). Finally, as a crystal ball in the heavens (79), the star of Mary ransoms us on the cross (84).

The enthroned Mary of Stanza 1 enters heaven on high in Stanza 3 (25). In Stanzas 4 and 5 she is established there as 'qwene serene' (37), 'hevinlie hie emprys' (38) and 'qwene of hevyn' (52). The dramatic cameo of the final stanza sets her beside God and Christ in 'Tryumphale hall' on 'hie trone regall' (75).

Later image lines are introduced slowly, so that the listener does not become confused. Mary as warrior on our behalf ('wicht in ficht') is held back until Stanza 3; as polished jewel of purity her entry is delayed until Stanza 6. But in the final stanza they all come together to signify divine harmony and mystery. The virgin's womb is the wall (73), the hospital (77) and the small room (78) protecting Christ the child in his vulnerability (73), but also the palatial suite (73), hall of triumph (75) and regal throne (75) suited to the sovereignty of the divine knight who fights evil on our behalf. Mary's own attributes also merge – in lines 79–81, earlier images combine to reinstate her as star-womb, rose-virgin, angel-mother. Wordplay contributes wittily to these evocations of mysterious unity. She (as well as her son) is our divine sustenance, at once filling full and fulfilling (80); she (as mother of her son) has a claim to have created the creator (82) and so to be our co-saviour (83–4), to be the originator of the divine originator.

Despite the phased presentation of the image lines, is this combination of high style, virtuoso versifying, imagistic counterpointing and metasymbolism not far too difficult for any audience, even a courtly one, to comprehend? Dunbar clearly does not think so, for he explicitly refers to the image of Mary as an *aide-mémoire* in Stanza 5. Telling her story in pictures will help the audience to memorise the theme of pain ('memore of sore'). The last picture of Mary in Stanza 1 likens her to a tree extending upwards from its root and branching outwards. This was itself a popular picture around which medieval people organised ideas and memorised them. It might equally well refer to the controlling or organising method of the entire poem. Repeated images form the trunk; they then gradually branch out referentially. Nor would the linking between pictures and ideas seem as idiosyncratic to listeners then as it might seem now. Different ages organise their thoughts in different ways and what seems an inconsequential movement to one may obviously fulfil the causal patterning of another.

For example, to a medieval audience, the call to remember

Mary's pain memorially would naturally have drawn in the associated images of her son suffering on the Cross and our own suffering which, ironically, He was expiating. If, in this case, the parallel patterning of ideas allows one image economically to suggest different penitential dramas, the same parallelisms allow apparently contrasted images repetitively to reinforce the same idea: the thornless rose, the tabernacle and the inn all signify the virgin birth.

History too may be imagistically simplified as the movement of the star within the time-scheme of the poem reveals. In Stanzas 1 and 3 it not only represents the Virgin; it rises in the heavens and descends into the east, thus recalling Shepherds and Nativity. In Stanzas 5 and 6 the star of dawn gives way to the moon star, signifying the life of Christ and the new age of Mercy. Finally, as the heavenly circular ball of Stanza 7, it completes that history in the Day of Judgement. Even that is not all; this ending in the star of Mary also concludes the day's natural cycle, the poem's formal cycle, the eulogising of God and the penitential counselling of man. One 'sign' thus extends its referential branches across metaphysics, natural science, astronomy, aesthetics, theology and ethics.

Medieval people had to rely on hearing words where we can read them. Literate and illiterate alike, therefore, relied on memorial devices a great deal and some people, in each category, were capable of prodigious feats of recollection.[5] We may be less gifted in this direction because we are less deprived but that should not blind us to different ways of organising thought. To omit this critical step in the specific case of 'Ane Ballat of Our Lady' will provide an interpretation which sees only the poem's labyrinthine complexity without picking up the threads which Dunbar offers as guidance through it.

When a communist, Hugh MacDiarmid, urges modern poets to follow the class-conscious, Christian maker, William Dunbar, rather than the people's poet, Robert Burns, it is clear that his preference is based on poetic rather than political criteria. This study of Dunbar's range of styles and effects explains what these are. He does have success in the homely, middle-style muse of Burns but, like MacDiarmid, prefers to move beyond it into the extremes of language and artifice as well. Additionally, even in the high style and structural complexity of 'Ane Ballat', he anticipates MacDiarmid's constant engagement in the practical work of poetic persuasion. In their most sophisticated modes and most arrogantly erudite moods, neither forgets the need to fashion an argument in ways which will accord with the experiences and thought-processes of their intended audience. The 'Seamless Garment'[6] of words woven by the one may have been designed in communist red for twentieth-century millworkers; the seamless verbal garment of the other may have been designed in Marian blue for fifteenth-century courtiers – but the arguments in each case are 'made' to suit the given group. For each of these Scottish lyricists, the art which conceals art was not enough, but an art which served art alone was pointless.

Suggestions for Further Reading and Study

(1) 'The Fenyeit Freir of Tungland', Personal Satire and Praise

Much of Dunbar's satiric verse focuses on individuals. These figures may also represent wider issues concerning the poet but the laughter is directed at a single person, known to the audience. (The method could profitably be compared with Burns – e.g. 'Holy Willie's Prayer'.) In Dunbar's work, study of the variety of satiric tones and the range of comic techniques employed by the 'maister poete' might, profitably, start with the close focus of these 'cameos': 'Complaint to the King aganis Mure' (p. 5), 'Of Sir Thomas Norny' (p. 63), and 'Epetaphe for Donald Owre' (p. 65). Poems of personal praise are less common but do exist. 'Welcome to the Lord Treasurer' (p. 49) and the two poems on Bernard Stewart – 'Ballade' (p. 130) and 'Elegy' (p. 133) – would open up this side of the enquiry.

(2) Timor Mortis Conturbat Me: Lamenting Mortality

'Lament for the Makaris' tends to be discussed in isolation because it, alone among Dunbar's verse, charts a mini-history of Scottish literature. But it belongs to a group of poems in which – thoughtfully, desperately or triumphantly – James IV's 'master poet' considers the problems of life under the shadow of death. Most (though not all) of these poems are tonally restrained and use the middle style consistently. It is especially important to look at such works precisely because Dunbar in virtuoso mood is so brilliant, the dance of complex rhymes and words on the page so eye-catching, that his thoughtful, understated verse can be overlooked. The quietly melancholic voice adopted in 'Of the Changes of Lyfe' (p. 140) could be compared with the more intense world-weariness shown in 'Of Manis Mortalitie' (p. 149) and 'All Erdly Joy Returnis in Pane' (p. 145), or the comfortless brevity of the ironically entitled 'Of Lyfe' (p. 151). Does religious comfort have any power in these poems, as – more obviously – in 'No Tressour Availis without

Glaidnes' (p. 148)? What view of the world is here suggested? Reconsideration, at this stage, of a poem discussed in Chapter One – 'Of the Warldis Vanitie' (p. 150) – might be useful. (Drummond of Hawthornden could be thought of as one of Dunbar's most talented Scottish disciples in this poetic mode.)

(3) 'Ane Ballat of Our Lady', Religious Verse and Decorum

The high style is not automatically chosen for religious verse. If one is concentrating, say, on the weaknesses of fallen man rather than the glory of God on high, a lower register is likely. Nor should one assume that once a stylistic level has been chosen, the poet will never depart from it. With these considerations in mind, it would be interesting to compare the aureate language of 'Ane Ballat of Our Lady' with that used in 'Quhen the Governour Past in France' (p. 139). Why is a poem with such a title[7] presented in the high style? If one then studies Dunbar's treatment of three crucial Christian dramas – 'Of the Nativitie of Christ' (p. 154), 'Of the Passioun of Christ' (p. 155), and 'On the Resurrection of Christ' (p. 159) – a contrasted question arises. Why is Christ apparently unworthy of the same sustained aureation? In trying to reach a view on this, three further questions may be posed. What are these works actually about? Is the high style completely eradicated in all of them? In what sense, if any, may Dunbar's choice of language be thought appropriate for their different forms and modes – the chorus of praise presented in the first; the penitential dream form and dramatic setting of the second; or the image-centred battle cry of the third?

Notes

1. p. 212, *The Poems of William Dunbar*, edited by W. MacKay MacKenzie, Mercat Press, 1990.
2. The basic form rhymes aaabcccb. It is later used as the norm for the Vice characters in David Lindsay's *Ane Satyre of the Thrie Estaitis*. James VI in 1585 gave the name 'cuttit or brokin' to any stanza containing longer and shorter line lengths.
3. There is no doubt that the narrator is meant to represent Dunbar.
4. The virgin birth.
5. See Mary Carruthers, *The Book of Memory* (Cambridge, 1990).
6. The reference is to MacDiarmid's poem of that name in which he uses weaving terminology to move the millworkers of Stobo from the mysteries of intertwining threads to the intertwining of ideas.
7. It is worth reiterating that some of the titles in MacKay MacKenzie's edition are his own invention and that many of the others may have been inserted by the scribes or copyists. In this case, however, the title could scarcely have been derived from the poem's content.

CHAPTER FOUR

Form and Meaning: Of 'Targe' and 'Tretis'[1]

In Chapter Three, I argued that 'unnatural contrivance is the highest aim of late medieval rhetorical theory' and used the three stylistic registers to explain this. In this chapter, I shall continue the study of those literary conventions which distance art from life, but this time focus on the relation between form and meaning.

One of the most popular poetic guidebooks available at the time was Geoffrey of Vinsauf's *Poetria Nova*. It taught the versifier to avoid the chronological arrangement of poetic material in which 'things and words follow the same sequence'.[2] This *ordo naturalis* or natural order was inferior because it was (i) too easy, (ii) too natural and (iii) too limited. 'The poem follows the pathway of art if a more effective order' is followed. After all, while the natural ordering 'has no offshoots; the second is prolific' and so the 'deft' craftsman may adapt any one of its possible orderings to his topic instead of being forced to follow the past-present-future succession of life.

Vinsauf's arguments were derived from the idea of poetic 'making'. 'If a man has a house to build, his impetuous hand does not rush into action. The measuring line of his mind first lays out the work, and he mentally outlines the successive steps in a definite order. The mind's hand shapes the entire house before the body's hand builds it.' That is, one works out the overall form first.

Modern readers have most trouble with this planned view of art when it is applied to emotional subjects. When art translates passion coldly, in terms of set conventions, most modern readers are uncomfortable, sensing a dislocation between medium and message. The inclination is to think, 'This is insincere'. In fact, it is only a different form of sincerity, derived from the criterion of craftsmanship.

The two works I have chosen for this discussion are contrasting love poems. 'The Goldyn Targe (Shield)' mirrors the battle of love allegorically in ethical terms while 'The Tretis of the Twa Mariit Wemen and the Wedo (Widow)' uses worldly voices to satirise medieval marriage. They are both, by Dunbar's standards, long poems. His lyrics are often subtly organised, as the study of 'Ane Ballat of Our Lady' showed, but his skills in artificial ordering reveal themselves best when lyrical brevity gives way to more expansive narrative forms.

While there is critical unanimity on the excellence of the 'Tretis', not everyone agrees that the 'Targe' is so successful. The reasons for this dubiety are not difficult to understand. A poem which opens:

> Ryght as the stern of day begouth° to schyne   star of day (Sun) began
> Quhen gone to bed war Vesper° and Lucyne°   evening star; moon
>
> (p. 112, lines 1–2)

is formal in the extreme. The Latinate diction of the high style joins with the apparatus of pagan mythology.

And for what purpose? The central theme is so simple and conventional that one wonders why 31 elaborate stanzas are needed to discuss it. Dame Beauty enters, intent on punishing the dreamer, at line 146 ('Come dame Beautee, rycht as scho wald me schent'). Five lines later, Reason offers his bright golden shield as a defence ('Than come Resoun, with schelde of gold so clere'). The poem's 279 lines might cynically be summed up in four words, 'Reason fights sexual passion'. Little wonder that some critics find the prefabricated form standing in the way of living verse.

The retort that this is an allegory and thus concerned with ideas rather than living drama is not a fully convincing one. Basically, the art of allegory is twofold – the presentation of a hidden message by means of an overt one. In practice, this usually means telling a story in such a way that it may be re-translated according to the logic of another discipline. Henryson, for example, relates the story of *Orpheus and Eurydice* in such a way that it can be re-read in psychological, ethical and theological terms if one substitutes reason for Orpheus and passion for Eurydice.

The 'Targe' does not come out of such a comparison well. Its allegoric theme may be on similar lines to Henryson's but it is not cleverly hidden. As lines 146 and 151 illustrate, simple personifications rather than double narrative translate the drama conceptually. If this withdraws from us the excitement of discovering for ourselves the concealed allegoric meaning, interest in the literal drama is equally diminished by the poem's derivative nature. The 'Targe' relies so heavily on past authors and traditional forms that even a medieval audience with its great respect for authority might well have objected that it had heard all this already.

An initial outline of the plot will provide a roll call of these authorities. The nine-line stanza of the 'Targe', with its aabaabbab rhyme scheme was a common one for love themes; it had been used for that purpose by many earlier writers, including Chaucer and Henryson. The opening praise of dawn (Stanzas 1–2) imitates a known form, the *aubade*. The formalised presentation of crystalline

Nature (Stanzas 1–5) is a conventional means of suggesting the perfect order of God's universe, before man's fall in the Garden of Eden. It suggests that the work will deal with the mysteries of creation. Such a sight usually precedes a spiritually profitable dream and so Dunbar's narrator dutifully falls asleep (Stanza 6).

In that state, he imagines the arrival of a ship (Stanzas 6–7). This is another conventional device, associated mainly with pageants and courtly interludes. Large model ships were drawn on to the performing area. The procession of pagan deities which emerges from Dunbar's dream ship to sing and dance (Stanzas 9–15) would not have been novel for a noble audience, used to such performances.

Echoes, general and particular, from Chaucer's *Troilus and Criseyde* and *Parlement of Fowles* as well as James I's *Kingis Quair*, have been traced by scholars in this section. But the entire dream description is derivative. The most pervasive source is a French love allegory – *Le Roman de la Rose*. This had been translated by Chaucer. It provides the idea of two courts – one female (Stanzas 9–12) and one male (Stanzas 13–14). It also furnishes most of the personified female attributes which, one platoon after another, attack the frightened narrator within his dream (Stanzas 15–26). Only at this stage does the 'targe' or shield of the title appear to defend him (Stanza 17). This motif belongs to the classical tradition of the 'psychomachia' (battle for the soul), as practised just before Dunbar by the English poet, Lydgate, in *Reson and Sensuallyte*.

The shield serves the dreamer well (Stanzas 17–20) but finally proves inadequate (Stanzas 21–25), handing him over to Hevynesse (Melancholy) in Stanza 26. He then awakes in obedience to the demands of the dream vision (Stanza 26–28) and modestly thanks his authorities in obedience to the rules of rhetoric (Stanzas 29–31).

If Dunbar had tried to conceal the derivative and mechanical elements within the 'Targe', one might quickly dismiss it as a poetic fraud. Instead, he goes out of his way to emphasise them. Indeed, the one stanza – Stanza 8 – which was omitted from the above account is an inserted piece of literary theory. It offers the rare chance to listen to a poet in his own defence.

>   Discrive° I wald, bot quho coud wele endyte°   describe; write
>   How all the feldis wyth thai lilies quhite
>   Depaynt war brycht, quhilk to the hevyn did glete°:   gleam
>   Noucht thou, Omer°, als fair as thou coud wryte,   Homer

For all thine ornate stilis° so perfyte;	literary works
Nor yit thou, Tullius°, quhois lippis suete	Cicero
Off rethorike did in to termes° flete°:	figures (rhetorical); flow
Your aureate tongis both bene all to lyte°,	inadequate
For to compile that paradise complete.	

(p. 114, lines 64–72)

In short, the 'Targe' is a high style ('aureate') poem which translates experience into the flowing rhythms ('flete') of verse within the artificial code ('termes') of Rhetoric as practised by such classical authorities as Homer and Cicero.

The last three stanzas of the work confirm these movements away from nature and life into the discipline of Rhetoric (29:1; 30:9). The line of authority passes from Greek and Latin to the vernacular tongue (29:2). Chaucer, Gower and Lydgate are admired not for what they say but for the way they say it. Specifically, their mastery of the aureate style (29:5; 30:2) which will enlighten *any* topic (29:5; 30:4–7) is praised. Self-evidently, these are not the terms by which Dunbar would wish all of his poetry to be judged. High artifice and high style are his aims for this *particular* work; they would be inappropriate for advice to merchants or when satirising fellow courtiers. His skills should, therefore, be assessed by judging how well he manipulates the form chosen.[3]

Those listeners who knew the poet personally would have an advantage. The Dunbar revealed in Chapter One was not at all modest about his art. The narrator-critic in the 'Targe', by way of contrast, oozes humility. If one applies rhetorical rather than psychological criteria, all is explained. To proclaim lack of skill was an acknowledged convention, known as the 'modesty topos'. It was usually placed at the start or, as here, at the end of a poem. The writer says he is only a rough craftsman but does so in an extremely sophisticated way. Dunbar appears to offer his audience a short, humble, simple book (31:1–2) lacking rhetorical skills (31:4–9). In fact his aureate language and complex stanza form, when translated into the very terms he feigns to reject, argue the opposite case.

Proving that an area of authorial intent is skilfully explicated does not necessarily guarantee enjoyment. One can applaud something for being good without being thrilled by it. In suggesting that the 'Targe' is a virtuoso effort, Dunbar offers to his knowledgeable audience ('eviry connyng wicht', 31:3) the pleasures which derive from seeing technical difficulties overcome. What his critical commentary on his own poem does forbid is qualitative condemnation on grounds other than those he has defined. To say that the 'Targe' does not please you because it lacks narrative excitement is a perfectly acceptable expression of personal taste. To say that it is a bad poem because it lacks a story, when the reasons for that omission have been explained, is weak criticism because it blames the artist for failing to achieve something he denies attempting.

Dunbar's statement of rhetorical intent suggests that he is following the guidelines of Vinsauf and others and so has 'shaped the entire poetic house' first. If one thinks in this way, and looks at the overall structure of the 'Targe', it soon becomes clear that the story has three different sections and that these have been artificially arranged to form three concentric circles:

(A) The narrator's descriptions of his waking state: Stanzas 1–5 and 28.
(B) His dream vision of the ship and its occupants: Stanzas 6–15 and 27.
(C) The inner dream-battle of the 'Goldyn Targe': Stanzas 16–26.

If this seems suspiciously technical, remember the building analogy. No builder or architect starts haphazardly piling bricks upwards without first devising a structure, at once attractive and suited to the precise needs of the buyer. The word-maker thought of his art in the same way. Therefore, in a work dealing with ultimate questions, the circle is actually the most obviously significant way of presenting the story-line. Critics suggested it for this theme, because it traced a perfect, unbroken shape, and so mirrored the deity. As the Christian God is three-in-one, three concentric circles simply advertise a more ambitious word-building of the sort a master-poet might attempt. The most basic rule of all is still satisfied – that form and meaning interrelate harmoniously.

(A) *Outside the Dream: Stanzas 1–5 and 28*
This, the outermost circle, is reminiscent of 'Ane Ballat of Our Lady'. In Stanzas 1–5, nature is once more illuminated; high style and clear image motifs dominate.

First, pictures of *awakening* are evoked. These are applied to all levels of activity and suggest that time is cyclical. The poet rises in springtime, the season of rebirth within the year's circle. He does so at dawn, the start of the day's cycle. Appropriately for a personification allegory, this is dramatised mythologically. Vesper and Lucyne, the stars of the night, give way to Phoebus, the sun, and Aurora, the dawn. Venus and May anticipate the love theme. Stanza 4 explains the world view, which permits personifications of nature to mingle with pagan gods. Everything in Nature is a reflection of the sun – 'That bewis bathit war in secund bemys Throu the reflex of Phebus visage brycht' (32–3). This translates the Christian idea that the temporal world is but a shadow of divine harmony. Within this scheme, the poetic perspective is moving slowly downwards. In Stanza 1, the poet was gazing up at the purple cape of the sun. By Stanza 5, he is seated on a mantle of roses[4] looking ahead of him at a natural landscape.

Secondly, bright *colours* abound. The green, white, red, purple, silver and gold landscape is that of crystalline nature, as in 'Ane Ballat'. Heraldic terminology – azure, gules – is also used, as in 'The Thrissill and the Rois'. The narrator, therefore, presents a literary and un-natural view of Nature even when awake. Nor do these colours appeal to the sense of sight alone. In Stanza 2, the sun tastes the silver drops of dew. In Stanzas 3 and 4, the song of the birds is heard and the referred heat on rose petals or riverside boughs is felt. Even smell enters the picture – literally – with the fragrant ('redolent') roses of Stanza 5.

The third image motif suggests the *divine* origins of all this. Nature's creatures are 'mery' (1:6), full of 'mirth' (3:1) and 'joy' (5:7) because they know this beauty signifies a higher, benevolent power. The birds draw in a specifically Christian ordering of the day's cycle by singing the canonical hours of the church ('houris' 2:1) as minstrels of heaven (1:8) and chapel clerks of love (3:3).

If one follows this artificial ordering, Stanza 28 becomes the next critical focus. There, the dreamer returns to his wakened state and Circle A closes:

28.	And as *I did awake* of my sueving°,	dreaming
	The *joyfull birdis* merily did syng	
	For *myrth* of *Phebus* tendir *bemes schene*°;	lovely
	Suete° war the vapouris, soft the *morowing*°,	sweet; morning
	Halesum the vale, depaynt° wyth *flouris ying*°;	coloured; young
	The air attemperit°, sobir and amene°;	mild; pleasant
	In *quhite and rede* was all the felde besene,	
	Throu *Naturis* nobil fresch *anamalyng*°,	enamelling
	In *mirthfull May*, of eviry moneth Quene.	

(p. 119, lines 244–52)

My italicisation highlights the major echoes between this stanza and the opening description of Nature.[5] The listener's memory is drawn back to the dramatic setting of the opening by echoes of the very words and phrases used to describe it.

Has anything changed? Two of the three major image motifs are firmly re-established. Mythologically Phoebus, Nature and May return to the stage. The illuminated colourings of white and red enamel are painted in again. From the divine perspective, God's world in Nature is still joyous and enlightened. But there is one variation. The specifically Christian image line of canonical and chapel clerks has disappeared. To discover why this is so, it is necessary to move further into the makar's circular building.

(B) *The Dream Ship: Stanzas 6–15 and 27*
The transition into sleep is poetically described by letting the sights and colours of the 'waking' landscape merge into the fanciful images of the dream ('my dremes fantasy' 6:4). The sail, which cuts the horizon and first suggests an approaching ship, is compared to the white blossoms of the springtime scene; 'A saill, als quhite as blossum upon spray' (6:6). The top of the mast ('merse') merges with the sun in a double imagistic transference, both elements of which echo the opening *aubade* – 'Wyth merse of gold, brycht as the stern of day' (6:7). The star of day is a simile for the sun which has the same comparative force in relation to the ship, which is, itself, a product of the slumbering imagination. Ever deeper layers of analogy convey the ever-deepening levels of consciousness.

The personifications used by the waking narrator to animate nature become the actors within this dramatised dream. The hundred ladies who disembark from the ship are 'Als (as) fresch as flouris... in May' (7:5). Male and female courts resurrect the pagan gods and goddesses of the opening section. New, more sombre figures appear. Beside Priapus, the god of gardens, stands the god of wildernesses, Phanus. In the female court, Fortune moves mankind up and down on her wheel; in the male court, the ever-changing wind, Eolus, blows us now one way, now another.

A sense of conflict and fear is building up. This is confirmed by the image employed for the ship itself. In the last line of Stanza 6, it emerges from the joyous, pious bird choirs as a single bird of prey; 'As falcoune swift desyrouse of hir pray (prey)'. This sense of doom transfers itself, tonally, to the narrator. His own moods vary, as if he is already under the control of Eolus and Fortune. His judgement is also called into question. Immediately prior to the new vision, he compares the 'hevynly' (15:6) songs of the courtiers to participation in a divine service (15:6). Yet these revels are led by Bacchus, god of drink, and Pluto, ruler of the underworld.

The fact that he is 'sudaynly affrayit' (15:8) follows from this confusion and is given retrospective force. He is paying a dear price for watching this spectacle, even now, when writing about it (15:9). The loss of spiritual certainty which distinguished Stanza

28 from Stanzas 1–5, is anticipated here and confirmed in Stanza 27. There, as the dream ship vanishes in preparation for the poet's awakening, he records a 'spirit affrayde' (27:8).

Circle B, therefore, opens and closes by confirming the tonal movement from joy to melancholy contrastively highlighted by the two sections of Circle A, which surround it. While the reasons for this are deferred to the centre of the structure, Circle C, both natural and artificial orders predetermine a tragic outcome for the battle described there.

(C) *The Golden Shield: 16–26*
If one thinks of the poem as a line from Stanza 1 to Stanza 31, its title seems odd. The golden targe only enters the action in Stanza 17. Formally, however, the shield stands at the centre of the three circles. It also represents the deepest state of sleeping consciousness, in which – according to dream lore – God might impart spiritual truths directly.

The battle, like all else in the 'Targe', is analytically developed. Venus initiates the attack on human reason. Such a god-creature conflict augurs badly for the weaker side. The shield as reason's symbol undergoes a series of assaults. Each of these is led by one allegorised aspect of love at the head of a troop of associated qualities.

Stanzas 18–20 face the narrator with a series of love experiences. In turn, he is tempted by Youth, by a mature woman (Suete Womanhede) and by a high class lady (Hie Degree). These characters and their companions represent different types of love experience but the order in which they appear also suggests a progression in time, from innocence to experience, youth to age.

Variations on the shield and arrow motif also make it clear that each assault is more dangerous than the one preceding it. When Youth attacks, the shield of Reason is not harmed at all – 'harmyt... no thing' (18:4). Sweet Womanhood tests it more severely with 'scharp assayes' (19:8) and High Degree lets loose a 'cloud of arowis' (20:7), so thick that it looks like a hail shower.

Only the final assault is successful. This time, the dramatic situation itself varies. The new features are: (i) Venus replaces Beauty with Dissymilance (Dissimulation) as commander. (ii) Allegorically, this signifies a change of tactics; the shield will face feigned virtue rather than the evils of passion undisguised. (iii) The new leader introduces her own warriors but also encourages chosen archers from the earlier conflicts, including Beauty herself, to return to the field.

The arrows 'rappit on as rayn' (22:6) as the shield is raised to protect man's soul. But this time one assault is immediately followed by another. The first 'schote of grundyn dartis' (23:1) is followed by a second 'aufull stoure' (23:4). It is conducted by dissemblers, so Presence (physical closeness) throws powder in Reason's eyes. Allegorically, this results in blindness and folly invading the soul of the narrator, who now sees Reason as a fool and thinks Beauty has assumed a new delightfulness. This accurately translates another feature of sleeping thought. He at once observes the battle yet knows it is his soul behind the targe. He is the one who has fallen into irrationality and will now carry his confusion sadly into the real world again.

When all the structural pieces have been fitted together, it might be expected that clarity of form would provide an equally clear conclusion. If three formal circles successfully 'sign' a poem, whose ultimate topic is the perfectly intended world of a God three-in-one, that same structure might also suggest, from another viewpoint, audience exclusion. And indeed the narrator, having completed the forward movement from waking state via rocks to ship to courts to targe, seems so determined to close off his neat poem-pattern, that he now puts the movement into quick reverse. It may take twenty-five stanzas to open up the three structural circles; only three are required to close them. The dreamer may hurtle back from targe to courts to ship to rocks to life and the waking state with unseemly haste but the design is exactly completed.

In fact, the analytic patternings of medieval and renaissance verse seldom close off issues because the rules of persuasive oratory, then current, highlighted audience involvement. In rushing to wrap up the mechanisms of his tale, Dunbar sacrifices formal balance for good, 'persuasive' reasons. The audience of the 'Targe' are, themselves, catapulted into a series of uncomfortable realisations. Their guide has lost his way and his vision, become a victim of Melancholy (26:2) and is now inordinately anxious to escape from the issues he has raised into the conventions of his art.

One major question, in particular, has been 'craftily' left unresolved and it is one which demands an answer from each and every individual, then and now, for his or her life. Do we accept the inevitability of our fallen state and fall to Venus *or* do we stand idealistically above the conflict *or* do we share the confused ground of the waking poet? The 'Targe' may not live as a story for some but its ideas are of vital relevance to all.

To move from 'Targe' to 'The Tretis (Story/Narrative) of the Twa Mariit Wemen and the Wedo' is to remain with the theme of love but exchange the indirectness of allegory for the directness of satirical invective.[6] Both have intricate structures, which are cleverly adapted to contrasted concerns within that broad topic. In a chapter headed 'Form and Meaning' it is advisable to establish what the new topic is before considering its poetic presentation.

The 'Tretis' is concerned with medieval marriage. In the Middle Ages, this tended to be an economic arrangement, in which women became part of the land-deal.[7] As warfare also dominated and men of all classes were called away from home for long periods, absence provided an opportunity, especially for noble ladies, to look elsewhere. The romanticised code of courtly love, which grew up, offered a model of behaviour to fill that gap. Passionate, idealised, secret and adulterous, it transferred sovereignty in love from man to woman. In considering the institution of marriage, Dunbar's characters have this vision as an alternative model.

How does Dunbar organise his material? The 'Tretis' is a debate in which four voices are heard. Of these, the narrator's opens and closes the poem. If he controls the narrative, the widow dominates the central debate. As mistress of ceremonies, she invites comments on that institution from a wife whose husband is old and impotent, then from one whose youthful partner misleadingly appears to be virile but, in practice, is no more satisfying. Having permitted them full comment, she introduces her own views. Having been twice married and twice widowed, she knows how to manipulate men both as wife and as free agent.

In the 'Targe', although the three circles of argument did not remain entirely separate, the different sections were analytically distinct. To imitate that conceptual structure by following the formal divisions in the critical response was appropriate. The 'Tretis', however, works on an interlinking principle known, rhetorically, as *concatenatio*. Moreover, while it shares the enthusiasm for conventions demonstrated in the 'Targe', the former are more often employed to frustrate the expectations they arouse than confirm them.

To match critical form appropriately to meaning, I shall set out the 'artificial order' first but follow the 'natural order' of the poem in the critical analysis.[8] This enables the traps which Dunbar set for first-time listeners to be recaptured without losing the opportunity to observe the way in which similar voices may be interlinked although distant from one another within the poetic line.

In the outline below, the line numbers are consecutive while the letters distinguish the major narrative modes. In broad terms, we are about to hear a debate about marriage in which three different kinds of narrative are employed. In the table below, the letters call attention to this pattern.

Ai/Aii: The narrator's *inner thoughts* open and close the discussion
Bi/Bii/Biii: One character – the widow – is Convenor of the Debate and so provides three brief *introductions to speaker and topic*
Ci/Cii/Ciii: The three long *speeches*, which form the body of 'tretis', are given in turn by the First Wife (Ci), the Second Wife (Cii) and by the widow herself (Ciii).

To follow the consecutive story line (natural order) while remaining aware of the parallel patternings (artificial order) is, we have learned, what the literary critics of the day urged and the best makars of the day practised. If the specific organisation described above and set out in the diagram below is, indeed, close to the way in which Dunbar constructed his poem, then, following it should help us to understand why this particular form is especially appropriate for this particular theme or argument. It should also provide us with an answer to two further questions. Why does the story-line begin and end with contributions from the narrator, each giving us an insight into his expectations and worries? What persuasive or explicatory function is served by setting the speeches of three very different women within such a clear-cut, parallel structure?

Line		Major Voice	Content
Ai	1–40	Narrator	The scene is set
Bi	41–8	Widow	The stage is set for First Wife
Ci	49–145	First Wife	The complaint against age
Bii	146–57	Widow	The stage is set for Second Wife
Cii	158–238	Second Wife	The complaint against maturity
Biii	239–250	Widow	The stage is set for herself
Ciii	251–504	Widow	The issues are resolved
Aii	505–31	Narrator	The scene is re-set

Ai. *Lines 1–40: The Narrator sets the Scene*
It would appear that the world of the 'Goldyn Targe' is to be revived:

> I hard, under ane holyn hevinlie grein hewit,
> Ane hie speiche, at my hand, with hautand wourdis;
> With that in haist to the hege so hard I inthrang
> That I was heildit with hawthorne and with heynd leveis:
> Throw pykis of the plet thorne I presandlie luikit,
> Gif ony persoun wald approche within that plesand garding.
>
> (p. 85, lines 11–16)

> [Under a holly tree, heavenly green in colour, I overheard near at hand loud talk employing haughty words; thereupon, I hurried and thrust myself into the hedge so forcefully, that I became tightly entangled in the hawthorn leaves. Presently, I looked out through the intertwined spikes of thorn to see if anyone would enter that pleasant garden.]

The Latinate and compound words establish the high style. As the poet hides himself (in obedience to the conventions of the *chanson d'aventure* mode) his own listeners have been stylistically and modally conditioned to expect an uplifting tale of noble ladies.

The opening scene, in 'Tretis' as in 'Targe', appeals overtly to the senses of sound and sight. Nature is joyous, harmonious, brightly coloured and gleaming as are the flowers of womanhood who adorn it:

> I saw thre gay ladeis sit in ane grene arbeir,
> All grathit in to garlandis of fresche gudlie flouris;
> So glitterit as the gold wer thair glorius gilt tressis,
> Quhill all the gressis did gleme of the glaid hewis;
> Kemmit war thair cleir hair, and curiously sched
> Attour thair schulderis doun schyre, schyning full bricht.
>
> (p. 85, lines 17–22)

> [I saw three lively ladies sitting in a verdant garden, all of them arrayed in garlands of lovely, fresh flowers; their glorious, golden tresses glittered so much like gold wire that all the green plants glinted with the bright colours. Their fair hair was combed out and carefully parted, flowing down in a very bright cascade from their shoulders.]

It seems the courtly expectations were justified, although one discordant note may be detected. The setting of the drama on Midsummer's Eve, 'mirriest of nichtis', when anarchic forces were thought to rule, might cause an astute listener to be wary about assuming too much too early.

Only as the details of the scene are filled in does this 'lower' vision begin to take over. These noble ladies, if indeed they are noble, are not sipping their wine and talking quietly. Their manners are wanton and their speech indiscreet:

> Thay wauchtit at the wicht wyne and waris out wourdis;
> And syne thai spak more spedelie and sparit no matiris.
>
> (p. 86, lines 39–40)

[They took deep draughts of the strong wine and drawl out their words slowly; and then they began to speak at a faster pace and excluded no topics at all.]

The heavy alliteration of the low style invades the poem to describe characters who seem to belong to the world of Chaucer's bawdy miller rather than that of his 'perfect' knight. What has happened to the safe modal world of the *chanson d'aventure* and the reassuring setting of God's 'golden' world?

Bi. *Lines 41–48: The Widow introduces the First Wife*

> 'Bewrie,' said the Wedo, 'ye woddit wemen ying,
> Quhat mirth ye fand in maryage, sen ye war menis wyffis.'
>
> (p. 86, lines 41–2)
>
> ['Reveal,' said the Widow, 'you young married women, what mirth you have found in marriage since you became men's wives.']

This direct question from the widow replaces one French love mode with another – the lyrical *chanson d'amour* gives way to the drama of the *demande d'amour*. In this form, a question about love was posed and debated. As the widow suggests marriage as a topic, the poem's language decorously drops from high to middle style in accordance with the new mode and theme.

In setting the terms of the debate and handing over to the First Wife, the widow stresses that free speech is the only order of the evening. The image she offers in Middle Scots is that of the wedding 'band', which can refer either positively to the ring or negatively to the bondage it may signify. 'Think ye it nocht ane blist band that bindis so fast?' Don't you consider it a blessed band which binds so closely? (47), she asks. Dunbar's chairperson is too wise to show her hand before discussion begins.

Ci. *Lines 49–145: The Case of the First Wife*
What does the First Wife think of marriage to an old man?

> I have ane wallidrag, ane worme, ane auld wobat carle,
> A waistit wolroun, na worth bot wourdis to clatter;
> Ane bumbart, ane dron bee, ane bag full of flewme,
> Ane skabbit skarth, ane scorpioun, ane scutarde behind;
> To see him scart his awin skyn grit scunner I think.
> Quhen kissis me that carybald, than kyndillis all my sorow;

>   As birs of ane brim bair, his berd is als stif,
>   Bot soft and soupill as the silk is his sary lume ...
>
>   (p. 87, lines 89–96)
>
> [I have a worthless fellow, a worm, an old caterpillar churl, a wasted wild boar, only suited to rattle out words; a lazy hummer, a drone bee, a bag full of phlegm, a scabby rascal, a scorpion, a skitterer at the rear. I think it scunnersome to see him scratching his own skin. When that rogue kisses me, then all my sorrow kindles up – his beard is as stiff as the bristles of a fiery boar but his sorry tool (penis) is as soft and supple as silk.]

Not much, it would appear.

This speech moves the poem's diction another step down. It is the low style suited to vituperation and flyting. She does not organise her nastiness but hurls her insults like brickbats. Before this, she has echoed and re-interpreted the phraseology of the widow's challenge. She has no doubt which of the two senses of wedding-'bond' she believes, rejecting 'ring' in favour of 'bondage'.

>   It, that ye call the blist° band that bindis so fast,   blessed
>   Is bair° of blis, and bailfull° ...   bare; wretched
>
>   (p. 86, lines 50–1)

She also moves swiftly from the general theme of marriage to her own experience of it. The widow may have asked, 'What do you think of the institution?' The First Wife replies, 'I hate my husband.'

Linguistically, this old man is converted into various repulsive forms of animal life. To the worm, caterpillar, bee, boar and scorpion references cited above, his wife adds comparisons to a bristly old hedgehog (107) and a diseased horse (114). Each image is justified by the desired insult of the moment. The hedgehog is needed to explain how his beard scratches her cheeks, the horse whinnying at a mare to suggest the old man leering at his wife. Inconsistency is no more a concern of her unrestrained fancy than logic is a concern in any flyting. She can as easily describe her faithlessness while blaming her husband for suspecting it, as she can visualise him as both worm and boar.

Other repulsive image lines reinforce her physical horror. Similes and metaphors drawn from the medieval death lyric emphasise his decayed state. She even fancifully transfers him to the other world as a devilish spirit before he has had the good grace to die of his own accord:

> With goreis his tua grym ene ar gladderit all about,
> And gorgeit lyk twa gutaris that war with glar stoppit;
> Bot quhen that glowrand gaist grippis me about,
> Than think I hiddowus Mahowne hes me in armes.
>
> (p. 87, lines 98–101)
>
> [His two grim eyes are filthily smeared all around and engorged like two gutters stuffed up with slime; but when that glowering ghost grips me, then I think hideous Mahomet[9] embraces me.]

Dunbar sustains her hatred through the quick, alliteratively pointed rhythms of the flyting mode. For the serene joys described by the narrator or the measured options offered by the widow, the First Wife substitutes a torrent of exquisitely visualised viciousness. It destroys the old man but its unrelieved maliciousness does not leave the orator entirely spotless either. Those listeners who have been uncritically carried along by her infectious enthusiasm will later have the practical and spiritual weaknesses implicit in her case teased out for them by the widow and by the narrator.

Bii. *Lines 146–57: The Widow introduces the Second Wife*

The image of teasing out one strand of wool is a helpful one. The rhetorical principle of 'concatenation' which controls the argument of the 'Tretis' implies that words, phrases, images and arguments are intertwined. Verbal and syntactic echoing underlines this. When encouraging the First Wife to open the discussion, the widow sought to discover, 'Quhat mirth ye fand in maryage?' (Bi/42). Her companion faces the same question. The widow only alters 'What' to 'How' and finds an alternative form for 'maryage'. With *matrimony ... How* haif ye farne (fared)?' (Bii/153–4). This echoing encourages listeners to remember and compare the last time the widow spoke.

The re-introduction of the word 'bond' has the same effect. However, the widow's invitation to decide, 'That band to blise, or to ban (curse), quhilk yow best thinkis' (Bii/154), not only echoes her own words (Bi/47), it also picks up verbally from the First Wife's interpretation of them in Ci/50–1. In this way, the technique binds together both sequential and parallel passages. Those who believe that Dunbar just happened to employ bonding mechanisms in a poem which turns on possible meanings of the word 'bond' underestimate his craftsmanship.

As the poetic argument works in an overlapping manner, establishing both common ground and differentiations, it is important to discover what distinguishes the widow's invitation to the Second Wife from that accorded to the first. Dramatically, she confirms the procedure by, on this occasion, looking forward as well as back. She will end the debate with her own contribution. If the First Wife has the right to reveal all ('Bewrie': 41) and the Second to narrate without feigning ('but fenyeing to tell': 151), she also may tell the truth without dissimulation ('say furth the south, dissymyland no word' (156).

But the narrator has briefly anticipated her offer and cast doubts on her reliability. He describes her as having 'warpit... wordis' (150). In Middle Scots, 'warpit' might mean either uttered or twisted. Will she honestly intertwine her story or twist truth to suit her own purposes? In a poem about the hypocrisies implied by marriage either is possible, and words embracing more than one potential sense are an especially apt way of expressing dilemma.

Cii. *Lines 158–238: The Case of the Second Wife*

The Second Wife returns to the terms of the earlier debate at once. She too is anxious to declare the truth (158); she too has a long catalogue ('ragment') of evidence to present; she too substitutes the fury of her words for positive action, having also been ruled by her husband. She even echoes the First Wife's acceptance of the key word 'bond' in its pejorative sense:

> Now sall the byle all out brist, that beild has so lang;
> For it to beir one my brist wes berdin our hevy:
> I sall the venome devoid with a vent large,
> And me assuage of the swalme, that suellit wes gret.
>
> (p. 89, lines 164–7)

[Now the boil, which has suppurated for so long, will burst. To carry it on my breast would be too heavy a burden; I shall cast out the poison in a heavy discharge and relieve myself of the swelling that has grown so large.]

This image of bilious words painfully bursting out introduces further links between Second Wife and First. Husbands are still to be judged on physical criteria; their physical impotence is still matched by woman's sense of social powerlessness, and this wife will join her companion in lashing them with words.

But the overlapping mode of argument is also confirmed. The two cases are not identical. For example, while the First Wife had longed to replace her aged husband with someone 'yaip, and ying' (79), the Second Wife's husband fulfils precisely that requisite. He is both 'young' and 'yaip'; unfortunately he is just as impotent – 'feblit of strenth' (170–71).

The image lines, foreseeably, also overlap. Men are demeaned by both wives through comparisons to beasts and plants; the Second Wife's husband is like a dog who pisses on bushes (186) or like a once straight branch, now withered (210). The latter's situation, however, erases the need for her to reiterate images of physical repulsiveness. It is the conflict between beautiful appearance and the uselessness it conceals which lies at the root of her discourse and her heart (162):

> He has a luke without lust and lif without curage;
> He has a forme without force and fessoun but vertu,
> And fair wordis but effect, all fruster of dedis;
> He is for ladyis in luf a right lusty chadow.
>
> (p. 89, lines 188–91)
>
> [He has the appearance without the fact of lustfulness and life without fortitude; he has a fair shape without vigour, and manners without power and fair words without result (i.e. they do not lead to the deeds they describe); entirely useless in action, for women in love he is a veritable shadow of virility.]

These four lines conveniently introduce the Second Wife's distinctive argument and the diction used to express it. Her husband is a shadow of virility (191) because, in him, appearance belies reality. Images and figures of speech underlining this conflict abound in his wife's long, vituperative outburst. Indeed, he is himself just a figure ('syphyr' 184) with no substance. Antithesis is ideally suited to this form of contrast. 'He has the looks but not the lustiness; is alive but not vital, he has a comely form but no sexual desire; manners but no strength.' His fair words are set against his inability to turn them into deeds. Soon the two devices unite. Similes and metaphors become the poetic actuality and may, themselves, be antithetically opposed. Her 'gem' of a husband gleams like gold but proves to be only glass (201–2). Verbs of appearance – 'semys', 'lukis' – also infiltrate themselves into the poem.

These devices are designed to suggest that her case is worse as well as different. 'Scho that has ane auld man nought all (not entirely) is begylit' (199). At least, the First Wife knew what she was getting and was not landed with an apparent Adonis, who turned out to be a churl and a freak.[10]

Biii/Ciii.*Lines 239–250; 251–504: The Widow introduces herself and presents her own case*
The widow's dual contribution as a mistress of ceremonies and participant may be thought of as an attempt to transcend, comprehend, transform and invert the passionate cases presented by the wives.

True to the principle of concatenation, the Second Wife had ended her speech (235–8) by linking it to the widow's leitmotiv image of the wedding band/bond and the First Wife's example of the free love of birds. The narrator even reminds us of the opening setting (239–44). It is the widow, this time, who upsets all these reconfirmations by dramatically overthrowing her own debating mode and the democratic procedures on which it was based (245–50).

She will not discuss; she will preach them a sermon. Before opening her case, she specifically asks God to provide a moral theme, capable of piercing the perverse hearts of her friends. 'God my spreit now inspir and my speche quykkin, And send me sentence to say, substantious and noble; Sa that my preching may pers your perverst hertis.' (247–9). She will not join the debate. From the high ground, she will, both graciously and condescendingly, inform.

If this is her moral and theological case for demanding attention, she has a practical one as well. Like Chaucer's Wife of Bath, she justifiably claims greater experience. She has been twice married and twice widowed. This not only gives her a fuller understanding of the institution as a two-term prisoner, it also enables her to explain what escape from it means. Now, she has a bawd and can attract noble suitors. Indeed, she can claim to have embraced all ranks, literally, having moved upwards from the lower classes (first husband) via merchants (second husband) to the highest in the realm (as widow). Significantly, this comprehensive argument includes all three stylistic registers – low, middle and high – as well.

The widow is able to transform the thinking of her younger companions because, when in their position, she manipulated the marriage state to her own purposes. She accepts that arranged, commercially-motivated marriage contracts within a patriarchal society militate against the sovereignty of women. She does not accept that this reduces females to whipping the air, their husbands and themselves with words alone. Before she became free, she was enjoying illicit affairs and making her husbands pay in a variety of ways for their pleasures.

But she also, literally, transfigures their case. That is, she takes up the wives' favoured figures of speech in order to change their application. Here is an example of her use of animal imagery:

> Thought ye as tygris be terne, be tretable in luf,
> And be as turtoris in your talk thought ye haif talis brukill;
> Be dragonis baith and dowis ay in double forme ...
>
> (p. 91, lines 261–3)
>
> [Though you are as ferocious as tigers, be accommodating in love; and be like turtle doves in your conversation, although you have frail tails (i.e. are promiscuously inclined); at all times be both dragons and doves in dual form.]

Instead of comparing men to animals in order to demean them, she applies bestial characteristics to women in order to dominate. The double form of hypocrisy, lamented as a feature of male conduct, by the subservient wives becomes, for the widow, a way of maintaining female control. The clever wife coos like a turtle dove but acts like a fierce tiger, uses loving words as a veil for vengeful action.

In this way, she also strives to turn the world upside down. This form of *inversion*, while wholly suitable for the anarchic revels of midsummer's eve and for the literal, worldly level of her tale, is not so effective in the moral and spiritual areas, which she has also claimed. It is one thing to claim sovereignty over man, another to usurp power over divinity.

The dilemma may be illustrated by continuing to look at her use of animal images and analogies. The widow's major 'sentence' (248) or moral theme is the retention of power in a spirit of pride. When outlining her code of action she uses birds as a model. While her companions had used that image to imagine an unattainable ideal of free love, she uses it to explain how to gain control in the power-game of marriage. Women should crow over men like the cock crowing on its dunghill and imitate the proud trappings of the peacock and the parrot.

But, on her own evidence, she speaks under the authority of the Christian God on a theme he has provided. In Christian theology, pride is the sin of the devil. The widow may grant to herself the rôle of a preacher, but when she sees herself as a cock crowing over her husband or feigns to be a turtle dove (symbol of the holy ghost) in order to act like a dragon or an adder (symbols of the devil), she is subverting the holy inspiration which, initially, she had claimed as her authority.

In telling her pupils to be like an angel with an adder's tail (265–6), she makes the immortal and devilish side to her preaching explicit. The widow may literally triumph over the sins of the husbands and so mount an effective satire against the inadequacies of medieval marriage. That victory is comically gained within the fallen world on materialistic grounds. When she tries to move into the allegorical realm of ideas and ideals, tensions enter the poem. If denial of debate in favour of sermonising is the first modal sign of her own hypocritical inconsistency, her usurping of the 'legend' form (504) in her own favour is the second. The holy life at the centre of this preaching will not be that of a saint, it will be her own.

When she visualises herself at the centre of a crowd distributing love in a spirit of mercy, her model is that of the woman in the Bible, who tried to touch Christ's garments. But she did so to gain spiritual purity through divine love.[11] In this, as in all else, the widow can only offer the physical shadow of the spiritual power she claims. Christ offered spiritual healing to all he touched; she offers kisses. Even the image of Christ riding on an ass towards the holy city, Jerusalem, is demeaningly translated, when she imagines herself riding on her second husband to the worldly city, Rome.[12] While this is a perfectly proper view of her control in their worldly relationship, the divine application of the image, with no apparent sense of its parodic or even blasphemous undertones, suggests the limitations of her victory in overriding self-love.

Philosophically, the image of reason controlling the horses of the appetites has been used by Plato to symbolise reason's control over the passions. When the wife evokes that image, visualising husband number two as a subdued dray horse (350–8), the sociological implications of the image may again be appropriate – no longer does he ride her physically; she rides him mentally. But she also details, for the benefit of her female acquaintances, how painfully she controls his bridle and how demeaned he has become. The disdainfulness of this description replaces reason's objectivity with passion's pride. Once more, the literal triumph is confirmed but the claimed allegorical victory is called into question.

And all this has been done by proudly overriding the dialectical ground rules she herself set. In offering a *demande d'amour* to others but claiming a 'sermon' about the 'legend' of herself, she shows literary duplicity as well, sinning against the spirit of making, which was dearest to the heart of her own 'makar'.

Aii. *Lines 505–30: The Narrator Rounds Off the Tretis*
The narrator rounds off the debate literally. He returns to the romantic setting and the high style. Time and again his words echo the opening of the poem. This has a dual effect. Fittingly for a work about hypocrisy, it confirms that the outer appearance has not changed although our understanding of the truth behind it has. Lines 505 and 510 echo lines 12 and 35 so that the auditors may remember the setting and the noble speech of the ladies in the context of their own stylistic duping. Line 512 forms a bridge across the entire structure to line 10 through the repetition of 'dew' and 'donkit' but when first those words were heard, the dew's moisture seemed simply to fit the *aubade* form. Since then, love debate, flyting, the death lyric, preaching and saints' lives have all wrestled for modal power in a work which finally has aligned itself most closely with the *chanson de la mal mariée* of the Wife of Bath.

If the purpose of a complex structure is at once to suggest theme and facilitate persuasion, Dunbar has met the challenge on both levels. This poem on marital hypocrisy has, emblematically, an attractive, ornate shell and a worldly, bitter core. Its interlinked form of argument has been verbally, syntactically and imagistically underlined by the principle of *concatenatio*. That rhetorical figure literally means chained together and the word 'chenyie' (chain) has appeared regularly throughout the work as an imagistic alternative for 'bond'.[13]

The idea of the linked chain also confirms that the formal pattern suggested above on page 48 is indeed a cleverly organised vehicle for the argument of this poem in particular. The high-style circle of Ai and Aii hypocritically surrounds the debate. The Widow's introductions (Bi/Bii/Biii) confirm her overall control while the speeches of the three women (Ci/Cii/Ciii) are interlinked, yet form a continuous developing chain of indictments against males and marriage. If the sudden stylistic variation from the high register of Ai to the low (B and C) followed by the high again (Aii) 'signs' the hypocritical 'band' (= ring) of the poem; so the interlinked images and figures of speech shadow the overlapping 'band' (= chain) of the central argument. Two meanings of that one word, stored in the memory, could resuscitate its mode and its message for Dunbar's 'auditouris'.

As a final, methodological test, compare the four lines which conclude section Aii with the four which round off Ai; that is, lines 527–30 with lines 37–40. In both, audience security is upset. Lines 37–40 are those in which the ladies unexpectedly 'wauchtit at the wicht wyne'. Lines 527–30 have the same disruptive effect:

> Ye auditouris most honorable, that eris hes gevin
> Oneto this uncouth aventur, quhilk airly me happinnit;
> Of thir thre wanton wiffis, that I haif writtin heir,
> Quhilk wald ye waill to your wif, gif ye suld wed one?
>
> (p. 97, lines 527–30)
>
> [Most honourable listeners, who have given ear to this strange adventure, which befell me early in the day; of these three wanton women about whom I have written here, which would you choose as your wife, if you were to wed one of them?]

The poem, so far, has satirised medieval marriage, the idealism of courtly love, the husbands (by statement) and the women (by enactment). Even the narrator has at times become a source of comedy. The last laugh, however, is reserved for us, the audience. If we thought we were comfortably outside this drama, free to munch our medieval equivalent of popcorn undisturbed by the drama, the author will not allow it. This is a universal problem and each must find his or her own answer.

Little wonder, then, that MacDiarmid admired so ambitious and imaginative a craftsman. Dunbar as 'makar' has also been the unifying topic of this book. Middle Scots in the late fifteenth century was a well established, subtle vernacular tongue and the master poet brilliantly exploited its entire range. Yet, as Iain Crichton Smith reminds us, 'you can be the most brilliant word-manipulator in the world and yet not be a poet', if you do not feel strongly. In addition, you need to know 'that what you're talking about is something that is meaningful and important' to your audience.[14] Understanding something about medieval thought and the conventions of medieval literature helps to explain what Dunbar's themes and concerns were. It clarifies why his ideas, dramatisations and exemplary tales were of importance to his contemporaries but, for the most part, remain so for us five hundred years later on.

Only when you see lurking behind a golden shield in a dream the power of sexual passion to overthrow your own reason, restraint and self-respect, or when you see beyond a flying alchemist to the continuing wars between arts and sciences, hypocrisy and truth, good and evil, God and the devil – only then will the passionate, persuasive 'making' of William Dunbar unveil itself to you in all its power.

That end, when achieved, is more than worth whatever effort has been expended in gaining it.

Suggestions for Further Reading and Study:

(1) Dunbar, Women and Love

As a dwarfish 'pillie wantoun' with as bitter a tongue as any of the women in his 'Tretis', Dunbar was probably not the most attractive figure at court. And certainly, his most direct treatments of love and women tend to be ironic and frustrated rather than joyous. 'In Prais of Wemen' (p. 83) is a good touchstone. Does the poem really offer the unstilted celebration of womankind suggested by the title? Having decided your answer, a fuller range might be tested by exploring the bawdiness of 'The Twa Cummeris' (p. 84), the satiric tones 'Of the Ladyis Solistaris at Court' (p. 97) and the painted idealism of 'To a Ladye' (p. 99).

More formal treatment of love and marriage also abounds. Remembering that Dunbar was a professional poet, paid to adapt his work to different persuasive purposes and different audiences, you could try to answer the following questions. Can the 'The Thrissil and the Rois' (p. 107) be seen as the idealistic counterpart in patriotic hopefulness to the cynical vision of the 'Tretis'? How does the hidden meaning of the allegoric poem 'Bewty and the Presoneir' (p. 104) relate to that of the 'Targe'? How, too, is love of woman related to love of God in his verse? In this last case, Dunbar handles the topic directly in 'Of Luve Erdly and Divine' (p. 101) but also casts it in the form of a debate between birds, 'The Merle and the Nychtingaill' (p. 134).

(2) Dunbar, Drama and Debate

It is a commonplace of criticism that Scotland has little or no drama in the Middle Ages and Renaissance. While this is true – especially in comparison to England's especially rich tradition in those periods – poetry, drama and prose-narrative were not so clearly distinguished one from the other then as now. The idea of 'voices' (related to the idea of literature being spoken or sung aloud) produced verse in which narrative, lyrical and dramatic movements intertwined.

Those who lament Scotland's theatrical poverty in extreme terms also equate 'drama' with performance in a theatre, with clear scene divisions and allocation of parts. This is to underestimate the importance of other, less clear-cut performance modes, such as the courtly interlude, pastoral debates or pageants. With very few exceptions, we do not have enough evidence to say definitely which of Dunbar's works were intended for performance. The strong dramatic line in his work may, however, be reconsidered with these freer divisions in mind.

The most obvious 'dramatic' mode, repeatedly offered by Dunbar, is that of debate. The popularity of this form derives, to some degree, from the medieval educational technique of asking students to argue on both sides of a topic. The 'Tretis' and 'The Merle and the Nychtingaill' form a convenient bridge between 'love' and 'debate'. Among the many formal oppositions presented by Dunbar, the clearly dramatised Edinburgh-Stirling argument of 'The Dregy' (p. 56) could lead into study/discussion of the verse battle between Kennedy and Dunbar in their Flyting (p. 5); the farcical martial opposition of 'The Sowtar and the Tailyouris War' (p. 123) and the serious moral debate offered in the lyric series 'Of Discretioun in Asking' (p. 31), 'Of Discretioun in Geving' (p. 33) and 'Of Discretioun in Taking' (35).

If you then imagine yourself as responsible for James IV's court performances either in the 'theatre' of mind or classroom, and try to produce and direct the following, you will soon understand why some critics have argued for their dramatic status:
(i) 'The Goldyn Targe'
(ii) 'The Dance of the Sevin Deidly Sinnis' leading in to 'The Sowtar and Tailyouris War' and 'The Amendis to the Telyouris and Sowtaris' (pp. 120–7).

As Dunbar also describes actual pageant-performances for specific royal events, there is the opportunity to work from his own poetic account. One might, for example, 're-create' – from the evidence presented in 'To Aberdein' (p. 137) – the sights which met the inhabitants of that city when Queen Margaret paid it her first royal visit in May 1511.

Notes:
1. *Longer Scottish Poems, Volume One: 1375–1650 (Edinburgh, 1987)*, edited by Priscilla Bawcutt and Felicity Riddy, contains excellent editions of both poems.
2. *Poetria Nova of Geoffrey of Vinsauf*, translated by Margaret F. Nims (Toronto, 1967), pp. 16–24 (18).
3. See Denton Fox, *English Literary History* xxvi (1959), pp. 311–34.
4. The poetic link between heavenly cape and earthly mantle is made within the dream in Stanza 6 but the view and setting carries over from Stanza 5.
5. Compare: Line 1 with 1:3; Line 2 with 1:6, 3:2; Line 3 with 1:5, 2:7, 4:6; Line 4 with 1:9; Line 5 with 6:6; Line 7 with 2:3; Line 8 with 2:4; Line 9 with 3:1.

6. Full translations will be provided more frequently as the 'Tretis' is linguistically difficult.
7. Tom Scott, *Dunbar* (Edinburgh, 1966) p. 21. Chapter 2 has a discussion on marriage and courtly love. The rest of the book, while giving a lively personal reading, is not always critically reliable.
8. See Vinsauf discussion, page 38 above.
9. Used interchangeably with Satan in much of the Christian literature of the Middle Ages.
10. 'Freke', line 210 had both of these senses in Middle Scots.
11. Matthew 9:21; Mark 5:28.
12. This opposition between Jerusalem (the heavenly city) and Rome (the city of worldly power) was a commonplace in medieval literature.
13. See lines 53, 55, 366.
14. John Blackburn, *The Poetry of Iain Crichton Smith*, Scotnote Number 8 (Aberdeen, 1993), pp. 4–5.

ADDITIONAL RESOURCES

Audio cassette:

Poems of William Dunbar,
Scotsoun Makars series.

Available from:
Scotsoun
13 Ashton Road
Glasgow G12 8SP

These poems are selected and introduced by
Professor Edwin Morgan and read by various voices.

Of special interest is a complete reading of
'The Tretis of the Twa Mariit Wemen and the Wedo'.